Finding beauty in the Ashes

Out of the ashes, beauty shall rise

Rosie Rivera

WESTBOW
PRESS®
A DIVISION OF THOMAS NELSON
& ZONDERVAN

WestBow Press books may be ordered through booksellers or by contacting:

WestBow Press
A Division of Thomas Nelson & Zondervan
1663 Liberty Drive
Bloomington, IN 47403
www.westbowpress.com
844-714-3454

Unless otherwise noted, all scripture taken from the King James Version of the Bible.

Scripture marked (NKJV) taken from the New King James Version®. Copyright © 1982 by Thomas Nelson. Used by permission. All rights reserved.

Scripture quotations marked (AMP) taken from the Amplified® Bible (AMP), Copyright © 2015 by The Lockman Foundation. Used by permission. www.Lockman.org

Scripture quotations taken from the Amplified® Bible (AMPC), Copyright © 1954, 1958, 1962, 1964, 1965, 1987 by The Lockman Foundation. Used by permission. www.lockman.org

ISBN: 978-1-6642-0709-7 (sc)
ISBN: 978-1-6642-0710-3 (e)

Library of Congress Control Number: 2020918716

Print information available on the last page.

WestBow Press rev. date: 12/3/2020

Acknowledgements

I WOULD LIKE TO take this opportunity to acknowledge my Lord and Savior Jesus Christ who has changed the course of my life and has made me a new creation in him. If it had not been for the Lord where would I be? My faith has become effectual as I acknowledge every good thing that is in me in Christ Jesus. I know that in myself I could not have accomplished the things I have accomplished in my life, but I am not looking after my ability, I rely on his grace working in me.

> *That the communication of thy faith may become effectual by acknowledging every good thing which is in you in Christ Jesus. (Philemon 1:6 KJV)*

My Lord and Savior came to heal the broken hearted and to proclaim liberty to the captives. He is the one responsible for the changes in my life.

> *"The Spirit of the Lord God is upon me; Because the Lord has anointed me to preach good tidings to the poor; He has sent me to heal the*

brokenhearted, to proclaim liberty to the captives,
And the opening of the prison to those who are
bound; To proclaim the acceptable year of the
Lord, and the day of the vengeance of our God;
To comfort all who mourn, To console those who
mourn in Zion, To give them beauty for ashes, the
oil of joy for mourning, The garment of praise for
the spirit of heaviness; That they may be called
trees of righteousness, The planting of the Lord,
that He may be glorified. (Isaiah 61:1-3 NKJV)

Dedication

I AM DEDICATING THIS book to my loving husband, Robert, who has stood by me throughout the phases of my spiritual growth and is the one who encourages me to do things I did not think I could do. Thank you Robert, for always being there for me and encouraging me to do better and go further than I thought I ever could, you are the love of my life. I also dedicate this book to my Lord and Savior Jesus Christ who gave me the ability to succeed and the one who instructed me to write my first book. This book is a sequel to the first book I wrote, Stolen Identity. It's an update on my spiritual journey of where I was when I met the Lord and how far he has brought me in my spiritual walk, how he took the pieces of my broken life and gave me beauty for ashes. Thank you, Lord Jesus, you are everything to me, you are responsible for transforming my life and turning the ashes of the past into something beautiful.

A Message to You, the Reader

*E*ACH TIME I write a book, I write it with you in mind. My heart goes out to those who have been struggling with their own thoughts of failure and past hurts. I want you to know that God can take the ashes of your life and turn them into something beautiful.

Your past does not identify who you are. Yes, you might have messed up and I am sure the enemy is bombarding your mind with thoughts of condemnation. You might be thinking, if only I could change the past, things would be so different. You can go a step further, not only change it, but have it erased by becoming a new creature in Christ.

> *Therefore, if anyone is in Christ, he is a new creation; old things have passed away; all things have become new.* (2 Corinthians 5:17 *NKJV*)

You might be thinking, how do I do that? You must do what the bible says if you want to be transformed in your thinking, to be forgiven and have your past erased.

That if thou shalt confess with thy mouth the Lord Jesus, and shalt believe in thine heart that God hath raised him from the dead, thou shalt be saved. For with the heart man believeth unto righteousness, and with the mouth confession is made unto salvation. For the scripture saith, whosoever believeth on him shall not be ashamed. (Romans 10:9 to 11 KJV)

I trust that as you read this book you will begin to see yourself as Jesus sees you, finding your identity in him you will no longer allow the past to define who you are.

For we are His workmanship, created in Christ Jesus unto good works, which God hath before ordained that we should walk in them. (Ephesians 2:10 KJV)

Contents

Introduction

INDING BEAUTY IN the ashes is a sequel to my first book, Stolen Identity. The Lord impressed me to write Stolen identity while listening to the testimony of a young man who had been struggling with drugs. I had no idea how to write a book or what to write about. At the time I did not realize that in writing the book I was going to be releasing the pent up emotions about the pain I had lived with, my own struggle with the past and how the Word of God helped me understand what I was going through. I see in *(Genesis 3 KJV)* how the enemy was able to steal the authority God had given Adam and Eve and by disobedience to God's command they lost their identity of who they were, They believed the devil's lies thinking it would make them more like God when God had already created them in his image. The enemy is still at work stealing man's identity through lies and deceptions which we believe. In studying the word of God, we come to find out who we are in Christ and who our real enemy is.

Since the writing of Stolen Identity, I have come to the realization that there are lots of people going through the same struggles I went through. I believe that is why the Lord led me to write Stolen Identity. Now that I am free from the past, I can help others learn how to overcome their struggles and find their identity in Christ.

So many years of my life were wasted dwelling on the past so that I was unable to enjoy the present. I felt unloved, ashamed, guilty, and inferior to others, always comparing myself to others and never being able to measure up. Thank God that he was there to lead me out of the past and has given me a future to look forward to, every day with the Lord is a new day.

When we continually dwell on the failures and mistakes of the past, it prevents us from enjoying the present. I know where you are coming from because I have been there. I understand how you sometimes feel alone and like no one understands. I am not writing about something that I know nothing about. I have experienced feelings of rejection, bitterness, guilt and anger. And all the feelings that come from not understanding why we feel the way we do. I want to use my failures to become a bridge that others can cross to freedom and not a barricade to their success.

People who have been abused or rejected tend to have an anger on the inside they cannot understand. They feel like somebody ought to pay for the pain they are going through. It is not anyone's responsibility to make you feel good or make you happy. We cannot depend upon people to make us feel good, but we can take God at his word when he says our life can be different.

I understand how anger contributes to the way you feel, I myself experienced an anger I could not understand. I took my anger out on the ones who really loved me. I was experiencing feelings of rejection and all the other feelings that go with it. I even struggled believing God really could love me. It was through reading and studying the word of God that I came to understand my feelings and emotions and why I behaved the way I did. I was able to see and understand God's unconditional love for me and to understand the pain Jesus had to endure to obtain my freedom.

It was in a little country church in 1979 where I first heard the message that I could be saved and that is how I came to the Lord and my life began to change in many ways. I found a new life in Christ, but my life did not change overnight, the transformation took place one day at a time. The soulish part of me, which contains the mind, the will and the emotions was the part I still could not understand. I did not know it was the soulish part of me that was acting out of the pain I felt. It was hard for me to understand why I still acted the way I did.

When one repents of one's sin and accepts the sacrifice of the Lord's death and believes that God raised him from the dead one becomes born again. In one's spirit one is made new but the rest changes as we understand the word of God and we begin to do what it says. We are spirit beings; we have a soul and we live in a body. That is why we must grow in knowledge and as we do; the change begins to take place. Our spirit is made new at the new birth, but we must bring the other two parts of our being into subjection to our spirit.

I believe this book will be an eye-opener for many and they will be able to understand why they feel the way they do and find their identity in Christ.

My husband and I graduated from Rhema Bible Training Center (college) in 1991, at the writing of this book Robert and I are currently in transition in ministry. We recently had been ministering in a Spanish church for 17 1/2 years, before that we pioneered a couple of other churches which didn't go very far because we were immature and didn't know the things we now know, but thank God people were getting saved and many are still serving God in spite of us. In the year 2000 we helped in a drug and rehab center for men in Georgia where we taught the word daily and the word helped men overcome their addiction. God cares about the addict just as he does for everyone else. He recognizes that man is weak in the flesh.

Throughout the years, we have grown and learned as much from what not to do as from what to do. When training for ministry I would hear ministers say we can learn as much from what not to do as we can from what to do, but I didn't really understand it till later after listening and observing some things that were being said and done.

During the time we pastored, we were able to make trips to Nicaragua, Guatemala and Mexico to minister the word. When we ministered there, we experienced the peace of knowing the Lord was with us. There was a time when I feared going to another country especially to a Spanish speaking country or a communist country because I feared the unknown, but the Lord has changed that. The times that I have gone I have sensed the peace and presence of God with me everywhere I went.

In the past we had shied away from Hispanic churches because we understood the culture and the traditions which have been handed down by parents and religion. We were able to see firsthand how traditions of man can infiltrate the church and be mixed with truth. Traditions are hard to break especially when they have been handed down from generation to generation.

In 1995 we attended language school at Kings Way Missionary Institute in McAllen Texas. We wanted to learn the Spanish language more accurately. Learning Spanish was a trying experience. I did not realize the Spanish language consisted of so many verbs that boggled the mind. We went through a year of studying Spanish with no idea that one day we would have the opportunity to minister in Latin countries.

As we minister in Spanish churches, I now feel at ease. Having knowledge of the language and the culture made it possible to be able to teach in Latin countries, The traditions that are there come from a lack of knowledge, having been taught traditions by their families and passed on to the next generation. Looking back, I am thankful I can speak and understand both languages.

One of the things the Lord has put on our heart is to teach people about the danger of mixing our traditions with the word of God. To teach them to search the scriptures and compare their traditions with what the bible teaches.

The bible says, *man's traditions have made the word of God of non- effect. (Mark 7:13 KJV)*

That is why we must be aware of the danger of mixing tradition with the word of God.

Language school was difficult. At times I felt like the Lord had abandoned me somewhere between the former church we had pastored and learning Spanish. I asked the Lord, "where are you?" Why have you forsaken me? I just could not concentrate on anything other than verbs. I could not sense God, I felt like God was far away from me. The Lord gave me the assurance from *(Joshua 1:9 KJV)* that he was with me and would go with me wherever I went. It was the first scripture the Lord spoke to me in Spanish. Isn't that amazing? God knows all languages. Hearing it in Spanish when I did not know what the Spanish bible says, gave me the assurance that he was with me even when I could not feel him.

Mondays were our days off, so we would go to the beach at Padre Island for the day to relax and get verbs off our minds. Just being still and listening to the sound of the waves and feeling the soft sand beneath my feet gave me a sense of peace. The beach was secluded at that time of year and no one was around. Sometimes we would just sit and watch the seagulls flying overhead and listen to the sound of the waves as they came ashore, other times we would walk on the beach looking for sand dollars and seashells. Praise the Lord, we made it through! What seemed to be a curse turned out to be a blessing in disguise.

From pioneering two different churches to everything we have done; we have always had a love for people and a desire to become more profitable to the kingdom of God. The hard times and the good times have prepared us for the work God has called us to. We have not escaped the tests and trials of life. We have become stronger and have become overcomers through the things we have gone through. Many Christians fall by the wayside when tests and trials come to try their faith. It has been through knowing God and our faith in God's word, with the help of the Holy Spirit that we have continued to press on until we reach the finish line.

Once we decided to follow the Lord, we have never turned back nor have we ever wanted to do so. This is the best life ever. I always encourage people to use the tests and trials of life as stepping-stones not as stumbling blocks, use them to propel you forward not as a stumbling block to hold you back in your walk with God. What an opportunity we have, to turn tests and trials into stepping-stones and grow in God's grace!

In 2017 we had the privilege of traveling to Bacalar, Mexico where we had the opportunity to get acquainted with the Mayan culture and to minister to them. Our missionary friends minister to thousands of children every year. What a blessing it was to see young people involved in teaching children and to watch those children loving and worshipping God. It is such a blessing to have had the opportunity to become acquainted with the Mayan culture. Ministry is all about people.

CHAPTER 1

God Finds Beauty in the Ashes

T HE THINGS I have been able to accomplish since my encounter with the Lord compel me to share with others how God took the ashes of my life and turned them into something beautiful. The day I met my Lord and Savior Jesus Christ was the beginning of my journey with God. It has certainly been an adventure. I determined since the beginning I was in this for the long haul, and I would not quit along the way. I've had mountain top experiences and I have been in the valley and I've had to fight the good fight of faith to stay in the race, but I am determined to see it through to the end and hear the Lord say, well done thou good and faithful servant.

Because of how God helped me through the difficult times in my life, I can now help you overcome things in your life because today I am a free woman with a desire to see those who have known the feelings of shame, humiliation, disgrace, unworthiness, anger and the pain of the past, find freedom.

When Jesus came into my life, he changed everything about me. He took the shattered pieces of my life and made them into something beautiful. It was not a painless process by no means. Like peeling an onion, he gently peeled off layer by layer. The first layer he removed was the layer of shame that dominated my life and the feelings I had about myself, then he peeled off layers of humiliation, guilt and layers of rejection and unworthiness, before he could get to the root of the problem. He helped me to understand what it was that caused me to believe that I had no worth and no value. Now I understand that we have an enemy who wants nothing more than to destroy God's creation. The devil is the one who condemns and places thoughts of despair in our minds. God did not send his Son into the world to condemn the world.

> *God sent not his Son into the world to condemn the world, but* that *the world through him might be saved. (John 3:17 KJV)*

God Never Gives up on You

Thank God that he never gave up on me. There were things that I had to do before I could be set free. I had to see and understand the underlying cause of my actions and my feelings of guilt and to be willing to endure the pain of the past no matter how painful it was, be willing to face the truth, be willing to deal with it, and most of all be willing to forgive and release those who had wronged me so that I could be set free.

God never gives up on you. The enemy is the one who puts thoughts in your mind that God does not love you, he has left you, he no longer has use for you. You must look him in the eye and say, devil, you are a liar and I will not listen to your lies. *The Devil is a liar and the father of lies. (John 8:44 NKJV)* He lies in order that he might get the advantage over his victims. You are not a victim of your past. You must let go of the victim mentality and replace it with one of victory. You can overcome because God has made you an overcomer.

Forgiving and Letting Go

Forgiving and letting go was difficult for me, because hurting people like to believe its everyone else's fault rather than face the problem at hand. I wanted everyone to feel my pain and misery. I was looking for sympathy, I wanted people to understand my pain without knowing what I was going through. I wanted them to understand my anger which I took out on those closest to me. I did not like myself. After I would blow up in anger, I felt condemnation, shame and guilt. I believed there was no hope for me. Feeling hopeless is an awful place to be because you feel trapped and it is difficult for one to see the way out.

Forgiving does not come easily. Some people struggle with it because they do not understand that forgiving someone benefits the one doing the forgiving more than the one being forgiven, although it also releases the one unforgiveness has held in bondage. Forgiving frees you from the tie to your abuser. Maybe that's why Jesus had to keep reminding the disciples to forgive not just once but seventy times seven. (*Matthew 18:21,22 KJV*)

There's an account in (*Matthew 18:21,35 KJV,*) about a servant who owed a considerable sum of money to his master and when he couldn't pay it, his master ordered that he be sold along with his wife and children to pay the debt. Then the debtor fell before him and begged him to be patient and he would pay all. The master had pity on him and forgave him the debt. Then this same man found someone who owed him less and he grabbed him by the throat and demanded that he pay what he owed. The man fell on his knees and begged him to be patient, but instead he had the man arrested and thrown into prison until the debt was paid in full. When the master found out what the servant had done to his fellow servant, not forgiving as his master had forgiven him, he was angry and had him thrown into prison to be tormented until he paid the whole debt.

This passage of scripture speaks volumes to me because I too have been in the throes of the tormentors of unforgiveness. All those feelings I was experiencing inside of me were making my life miserable. The thoughts would go away for a while, but they would always return to haunt me, I was not free until I understood about forgiveness and understood that forgiving was for my benefit as well as for the one who wronged me.

Throughout my years of ministry, I have encountered many of those living in pain because they refuse to endure the pain of the past long enough to face it head on and let it go and forgive the person who wronged them. When we think of the debt we owed and how Jesus forgave us our debt, it should inspire us to be willing also to forgive what others have done to us. No, it is not easy nor was it easy for Jesus to endure all the pain and suffering he had to endure for us, but he wanted to show you and me what great love he has for us.

I had a poor self-image. I was unable to trust and believe my life could be different. I was led to believe I was one of those labeled "damaged goods" and "beyond repair," who was looked down upon and unworthy of true love. I believed the lies that no decent man could ever love me. It took the love of God and my wonderful husband to help me realize that I could be loved by someone, that I had something to offer, and that I was not a lost cause. In God's eyes, I am his child and *born again not of corruptible seed but incorruptible by* the *word of God. (1 Peter 1:23 KJV)* I am loved by God. I have been accepted by him. My husband loves me and understands me.

When one believes there is no hope, pain, condemnation and regret can blind them and makes it difficult to see beyond the pain. It was hard for me to believe there was light at the end of the tunnel. I felt like there was no way out of my situation. I felt trapped and cornered because of my lack of knowledge and understanding of the word of God.

I wonder how many people there are, who do not know the Lord and are in the world with no hope, feeling helpless and alone in their misery.

I did not know the Lord at the time I was going through the things I went through, actually, even several years after my encounter with the Lord, I still found it difficult to believe things could change. I think of how different life would have been if I had known the Lord at an early age and how much pain I could have spared myself of if I had known the word of God or had someone who could minister to me without condemnation.

Meeting the Lord was the beginning of the changes that would take place in my life. I was amazed at how God accepted me and loved me just the way I was. That is how you come to Jesus, just as you are. He is not requiring that you clean up your life before coming to him. Come with your baggage, come with your fears, come with your guilt and shame. He will reveal to you the person he created you to be. The bible says he accepts all who come to him.

The excitement about being born again soon brought confusion because I noticed in the church that I was attending that women were not treated equally with men. Women were limited in what they could do. They were not allowed to teach men they were only allowed to teach children, they were never called upon to pray in public and it appeared that religion believes and teaches that women are inferior to men. Then I began to wonder and ask myself, is that how God sees women also? I had little knowledge of the word of God at that time, as much as I wanted to please the Lord, I wondered how could I be able to please a God who favored one of his creation above the other? Having had unpleasant experiences with men and doubts about who was trustworthy, I was not sure about trusting God. I know it all seems ridiculous now, but that is where my knowledge and understanding was at the time.

I was a baby Christian and knew little about the word, I did not know much about the character of God. I was inexperienced and limited in knowledge of what the scripture says. I had a lot to learn and a long way to go. Thank God for the hunger inside and the desire to know God. I spent endless hours devouring the word, learning who Jesus was and what he had done for me. When I became acquainted with the Lord through the word, I began to see a God who loved me even while I was yet a sinner, how much more now that I was his child? We can never stop learning and growing because God is so awesome, his word is alive, and his wisdom is far beyond mere human comprehension.

Becoming a Christian helped me find the answers I so desperately needed. I discovered the greatest love I had ever known. Knowing God loved me despite all my failures gave me the assurance that regardless of how I felt, I was not a failure. I was a success going somewhere to happen and so are you.

As I studied the word of God I was able to see that in the beginning God made man in his image, **male and female** he created them and gave them authority over the fish of the sea and the fowl of the air and everything that creeps on the ground and said to **them** to be fruitful and multiply and replenish the earth. The bible says God created **them** in his image, **male and female** not just the man but the woman also. (*Genesis 1:26-27* KJV) How different it is when you know the truth because the truth is what sets man free.

Studying the bible, I began to see a whole different perspective of God and who he is. I came to know a God of compassion, one who loves his creation and who is merciful. I saw in the gospels the way Jesus ministered to women. I saw him having compassion on the sinner, the adulteress, the widow, the sick, the one looking for love in all the wrong places. I began seeing God through my Lord and Savior, Jesus Christ.

> *Jesus said to him, "Have I been with you so long and you do not know Me yet? Whoever has seen Me. Has seen the Father. How can you say show us the Father"? (John 14:9 NKJV)*

I believed in God and Jesus as far back as I can remember, but I did not have a personal relationship with him. I knew about him, but I did not know him. I did not understand the bible.

Ministering in churches, many times I see the familiar look of pain on people's faces; I sense that they have built walls around their heart to keep the hurts out. I recognize those walls. They are the same walls I built as protection from my own fears of what people might think.

Fear is real, and it causes one to react in unhealthy ways. Fear wants you to run from something that is not chasing you. The bible says *God hath not given us* the spirit *of fear; but of power and of love, and of a sound mind. (2 Timothy 1:7 KJV)* The feelings of guilt and shame are so deep rooted in the soul of a person who has been hurt so that one keeps one's feelings hidden because of fear of being rejected.

Jesus came to set people free from the lies of the enemy. He came with an assignment from the Father.

> *Jesus said: The Spirit of the Lord is upon me, because he hath anointed me to preach the gospel to the poor; he hath sent me to heal the broken hearted, to preach deliverance to the captives, and recovering of sight to the blind, to set at liberty them that are bruised, to preach the acceptable year of the Lord. (Luke 4:18-19 KJV)*

One of Jesus purposes for coming was to preach the gospel to the poor, to minister healing to the brokenhearted, to preach deliverance to the captives, recovering of sight to the blind and to set at liberty them that are bruised. That sounds like the world we live in. Everywhere we look we see people in need.

There are many who appear to have it all together on the outside but inside they have souls that are in torment. They are crying out, asking; "can anybody hear me?" "Can anybody feel my pain?" "Can anybody see the real me?" Jesus hears you and wants to help you find peace in yourself, to throw off the shackles of sin and shame and break the chains that bind you, to demonstrate to you what real love is all about. He knows your every hurt and sees the tears you cry. Many people are crying in silence because they think no one cares but Jesus is listening, and he wants to comfort you, he wants to turn your sorrow into joy.

The Lord will never leave you; he is always by your side. He can always be depended upon. Knowing that Jesus is always with me has become a reality in my life. I can go anywhere he sends me, and I know without a doubt that he will always be there beside me.

I used to fear even the thought of going to unfamiliar places, but once I stepped out in faith, I felt an overwhelming peace because I experienced God's presence in knowing he was with me. The first trip we made to Nicaragua, I went with fear and trembling having never been outside the United States. I was shocked to realize I was feeling closer to God as we flew over the ocean and as we landed, all my fears and doubts disappeared as I was filled with a different kind of peace that I had not experienced before. It was the kind of peace the bible talks about, a peace that passes all understanding, that keeps one in perfect peace.

I wrote a poem in my book Rays of Hope that I believe you can identify with. **The shattered vase.** Throughout the years I have felt inspired to write poems which I put into book form to bless others with that which God has given me.

As you read this poem, I hope it will minister to you about how much Jesus loves you, how he was willing to come in the form of man to redeem us from our sin and make us new creatures in him. There are many shattered vases, with pieces scattered everywhere. Jesus came and gathered the pieces of our shattered life and made something beautiful out of them. I thank God that he did not leave me the way I was. I am thankful for his word that has transformed my life. One of my favorite sayings is, "God is good." I say it because I know he is good. I have experienced the goodness of the Lord.

God Wants You Whole

You are complete in him; you cannot be complete any other way. I know that in this age we live in, we are told there are other ways to freedom because you are your own person and you are free to do your own thing. Yes, God created us with a free will because he wants us to love him, worship him and serve him by choice and not by force. If the word of God did not give us boundaries to live by our world would be in a bigger mess than it is today. We can see where doing our own thing and having our own way is leading us. Jesus is the missing piece to the puzzle of your life, the missing link to bigger and better things. He has made all the difference in my life. I do not know where I would be today if I had not had an encounter with Jesus Christ. He is the best thing that ever happened to me. I am forever grateful for his love and faithfulness.

I wrote this poem because it describes me and how the Lord took the broken pieces of my life and turned my life around. I want you to experience freedom from fear of failure and freedom from the past. The Lord is the only one who can give you the peace of mind you crave for and an assurance that you have been forgiven. It's up to you to receive it.

The Shattered Vase

There once was a shattered vase, discarded by everyone, broken and battered, the damage had been done.

One day God walked through the rubbish to see what he could find. to see what was left of what sin had left behind.

He saw the shattered vase, pieces scattered everywhere. He picked them up so gently, with tender loving care.

As he spread them out before him, he saw rejection, fear and despair.

Sin left nothing good, it was so unfair! He took them to his Son and began to lay them out.

Abuse, insecurities, addictions, the pieces were all there.

Moved with such compassion! Jesus began to speak, "lo, I come to do thy will oh God, Hebrews 10:9 KJV, whatever the cost may be.

"I will go down to earth and set humanity free." A body, God prepared for him. He did it all for me and sent him down to die on Calvary's tree.

Bleeding on the cross that day, he hung between heaven and earth.

The road was being paved with blood, so we could have new birth.

I am so grateful for God's compassion and how Jesus loved me so.

I will never forget the words of the great commission "go."

Out there are many shattered vases, many broken reeds, sin and shame has taken its toll, but we have what they need.

I can never forget where I came from, I was that shattered vase. To the world around me I was an impossible case.

But Jesus came and saved me through a demonstration of his love.

The greatest gift one can receive is Jesus, God's gift from up above.

The Lord has given me poems about many different things. I just wrote them in a notebook and saved them until my husband talked me into putting them in book form. A few years ago, I put them in a book entitled, Rays of Hope, for those of you who love poetry.

I believe poetry is the language of the heart just as music is a universal language. I enjoy both. Poems can encourage when encouragement is needed, and music can gladden the heart and bring soul peace. It also is a way for us to express praise and worship to God and thanksgiving for all the wonderful things he has done.

CHAPTER 2

Having Eyes to See

Finding Beauty in the Ashes was Born

I HAD NO INTENTION of writing another book. It takes a lot of concentration and thought in the writing of a book, but I wanted to write this book to inspire you to be all you can be for God. My desire is to see all women and men set free and become the vessels of honor God created them to be. God takes the shattered pieces of one's life and makes all things new. He is in the restoration business.

Hurting People are Everywhere

Everywhere we go we encounter people with problems. I have an acquaintance who is having problems in her marriage. She talks about how her husband is constantly putting her down. She is the one who can never do anything right in his eyes, criticized for everything she does, unable to spend money without her husband being with her. She is a hard working woman who always keeps her home clean and her family taken care of, yet she is unable to please her husband or come out from under the bondage of feeling unloved and a failure at everything she attempts. That sort of relationship can cause a woman to see herself as unworthy so that she becomes intimidated and develops a low self-esteem. I asked if she has talked to her husband about it, but she is too intimidated to strike up a conversation with him about her personal feelings.

Abuse comes in many forms, such as domestic abuse, sexual abuse or verbal abuse. Many times, verbal abuse is more damaging than physical abuse, the scars of verbal abuse cut deep and produce painful thoughts and emotions. Statistics show that 12 million women and men over the course of a year are victims of domestic abuse; not all the abuse is physical and not all abuse comes from men. We know those statistics grow and increase year by year. Abuse can be emotional; it can be mental, physical or financial as well. It is so sad that the one person who should be trusted the most, the man or woman one married, is the very one who appears to cause the most pain. It is more painful when it comes from the person one loves. Built up frustrations are the cause of strife between a husband and a wife. Where there is a lack of communication between a husband and wife, there is a lack of understanding. Many marriages end in divorce because of a lack of communication between married couples.

Most of us do not realize how much words can hurt. The bible instructs men to live with their wives according to knowledge. (*1 Peter 3:7 KJV*) Lots of men are ignorant of what makes a woman tick. Hurting words go down into ones innermost being and wound one's spirit. I realize that women also say hurting words that can make a man feel less than a man. We are all human and many times those pent-up emotions rise and display themselves in anger toward the one closest to us.

> *The spirit of man will sustain his infirmity; but a wounded spirit who can bear? (Proverbs18:14 KJV)*

As I am ministering in churches. I see the pain in the eyes of people. There are many people who are walking around with a wounded soul. They are in the marketplace, at the mall, sitting next to you in church, sometimes they are in the pulpit ministering to you, some have learned the art of hiding their pain. Then there are the beautiful successful ones seen on TV who appear to have it all together yet deep down they are broken people. Some minister to the needs of others while hiding their own pain. Many movie actors are lonely people, they do fine when in a crowd but when by themselves the loneliness gets the best of them and they end up committing suicide.

Lord Give me Eyes to See

My prayer is Lord "give me eyes to see and ears to hear the cry of those who suffer in silence." Show me a way that

I can minister to them. Encouragement goes a long way and sometimes that is what some spouses crave from their husband or wife. Some go into marriage ignorant about many things and do not realize that we all have a need to feel loved and could use some encouragement from time to time. All humans long to be loved and appreciated.

I see the longing in the eyes of some women sitting in church, just wanting to be told by someone that they are welcome, appreciated and glad that they have come. Just one encouraging word can brighten up one's day.

I personally know a woman who is struggling to understand how she got into this place where she now finds herself. What brought her to this place, where did it all begin? Living here in West Texas in the middle of the oil boom, we hear of many accidents caused by careless drivers, some texting, some overworked, some fighting fatigue, and others are under the influence of drugs and alcohol. Many lives have been lost on our highways especially at the beginning of the oil boom because we must drive with extra caution due to the 18 wheelers on the highways and country roads. This young woman while driving under the influence crashed into a man on a motorcycle, failed to render aide and the man died because of it. She was convicted and had to spend several years in prison. It became a situation that could have been avoided but instead it resulted in this woman struggling to forget, not knowing how to deal with it. The thoughts and memories still run through her mind. She now suffers with guilt feelings and fear that control her thoughts. She is having to live with the consequences of her mistakes, but it does not have to be that way. God is a forgiving God who wants to help her get over the pain and give new meaning to her life.

There is Pleasure in Sin for a Season

The bible says *there is pleasure in sin for a season,* (*Hebrews 11:24 -26 KJV*) but that season always comes to an end and one is left having to deal with the consequences of one's actions. There are always consequences to every wrong that we do. When one is under the influence of alcohol or drugs, that one does not care about the consequences until it is too late.

The enemy will never let you rest; he is a hard task master. He suggests things that sound good, look good, feel good, then tells you just this once will not hurt, then entraps you through self-condemnation. The enemy wants to steal your peace, making you someone God never intended you to be. That enemy is the devil and he is mean and does not care about you or me. His own desire is to steal, kill and destroy everything that represents God.

We sometimes wonder why God is not answering us when we pray, but God is not going to do everything for us without us doing our part. The only way to be free from the trap of the enemy is first to allow Jesus to help you, to heal your heartache and your pain and then begin renewing your mind with the word of God. The word of God is like a mirror where we see ourselves the way God sees us. We must turn away from the old mirror which holds a reflection of hurt, pain and suffering and begin looking into the mirror of God's word and begin to see the reflection that God sees when he looks at us.

You must say no to the negative thoughts that bombard your mind and yes to what the word of God says about you. *(Read Ephesians chapters 1 and 2),* You are loved, accepted and adopted into God's family, created in the image of God. The enemy has flawed your self-image, he has stolen your identity, telling you that you are unworthy, if he can keep you believing those lies, he can keep you from discovering God's plan for your life.

> *The devil is a liar and the father of lies* according to (*John 8:44*. KJV)

You must not allow the enemy to continue depositing unhealthy thoughts into your mind. You must not allow the lies of the devil and the world to dictate how your life should be. The world is ever so quick to judge and condemn what they do not understand. We are not here to judge one another or to condemn, we have been instructed by God to love one another.

Do not be Identified with Your Past

What if I fail God after I get born again? You probably will, there are no perfect human beings. We all make mistakes.

What if the temptation to do the things I used to do still haunts me? What if I gave in and sinned and now, I do not know how to resist or how to get out of it? I do not want to do what I am doing but it seems like the harder I try to quit the deeper I sink. Can anybody help me?

It is not a sin to be tempted. Jesus was tempted in all points as we are yet without sin. (*Hebrews 4:15 KJV*) Why? He never entered in the temptation. God always makes a way of escape, but the flesh is weak, unless the spirit becomes stronger than the flesh, the flesh always wins. That is why we must be transformed by renewing our mind. Before coming to the Lord we followed the course of this world, we just followed the crowd, not being concerned about where it was taking us, but now that we know the Lord we are instructed in the word to be transformed by renewing our mind.

> *And be not conformed to this world: but be ye transformed by the renewing of your mind, that ye may prove what is that good, and acceptable, and perfect will of God.*
>
> *(Romans 12:2 KJV)*

What do I do now that I gave in to temptation? Is God mad at me? Does it mean I can no longer be restored? I hear voices telling me I really messed up this time, God does not love me, why even try.

Repent, thank God for his forgiveness, and forgive yourself and those who have wronged you, begin to fill your spirit with God's word, the word is your guide; it's a lamp to your feet and a light unto your path. (*Psalm 119:105 KJV*) You cannot continue to walk in darkness when your path is being lit up by the word. *Jesus said If you continue in my word, you shall know the truth and the truth will make you free.* (*John 8:31,32 KJV*) God's word is truth. God's truth will not only make you free it will keep you free. God is in the restoring business; the world is the one that discards one as a lost cause. There is a clause there most people ignore and that is, *(if you continue in my word).* It is only through the continual study of God's word that we are made free. God's word becomes real to us when we begin to see how applying it to our situation is producing change.

Now that you have been forgiven you must learn how to trust in God; do not see him as someone waiting to punish you for every wrong thing you do, for every little mistake you make. See him as your loving Father who loves you and wants what is best for you and is willing to take you out of your situation and give you a new beginning. The bible says in (*John 3:17 KJV*) Jesus is not the one who condemns. Jesus came to seek and save the lost, to heal the broken hearted and to set the captives free.

Man's mind is the battleground where our battles are won or lost and that is where the enemy has the greatest stronghold. The mind is like a computer, we must choose which thoughts give life and which thoughts bring death, delete the unwanted thoughts and replace them with life giving thoughts. It is a process which takes place by studying the word and understanding how to become a doer and not a hearer only.

> *So then faith comes by hearing, and hearing by the word of God. (Romans 10:17 KJV)*

If we look around us there are People everywhere who are struggling with their identity. Who am I, why do I have these unnatural tendencies, what is wrong with me? I personally know a woman who finds herself caught up in a relationship she does not know how to get out of. How did she get to this point in her life? Maybe it was because she felt accepted by a certain group of people while others rejected her. Maybe she felt she found the place where she finally fit in. We've yet to understand why certain things affect people differently; some find themselves on the road that leads to destruction in life because they were abused as a child while others become determined not to allow things that took place in the past to dictate their future. It is not wise to concentrate so much on the past that we forget the future does not have to mimic the past, things change, times change, and things can be different.

One of the greatest satisfactions in my life is ministering to women and seeing them set free. I can only do it by the grace of God that enables me to minister the word of God with conviction because I know where my help comes from.

Let us look at a woman in the bible that was looking for love in all the wrong places and found out why relationships were not the answer she needed. Let us get into some teaching of the word.

The Woman at the Well

> *There cometh a woman of Samaria to draw water; Jesus saith unto her, Give me to drink. (John 4:7 KJV)*

Read *(John 4:8-24 KJV)* for the following scriptures relating to the woman at the well.

Who is this woman? She is a Samaritan. What brought her to this place? It makes one question, what kind of childhood did this woman have? People tend to blame the way they were raised as the reason why they act like they do. What kind of environment did she grow up in and why did she marry several times, how and why did those marriages end? Was there abuse? Whose fault was it? Why did the marriage break up? Why did she seek another relationship after the first failed? Was she trying to find love in all the wrong places, making one mistake after another, maybe her husbands died but why? She had to be seeking something she had not found in relationships.

It was the sixth hour of the day or around 12 o'clock, the other women had already been to the well filling their water pots, was she hiding somewhere waiting till everyone left, looking around, trying to avoid the snickers of the people, the accusations, the stares, the looks of contempt? Was she a woman the world judged unworthy and looked down on?

She had five husbands and now was living with a man she was not married to; you can be sure there was gossip. People are cruel; they seem to see the speck in someone's eye while ignoring the log in their own eye.

She walks up to the well with such caution. Did she even notice the man sitting on the well? Suddenly a man talks to her, asks her to give him a drink. She turns to see this man sitting at the well, there was something different about this man, was it the gentle way he spoke? He was kind and spoke softly, and he was a Jew. How strange it must have seemed for this man to be speaking to her, a Samaritan. Jews did not speak to Samaritans so why was he asking her for a drink. Why didn't he ask one of the other women who came to draw?

Jesus speaks to her and tells her that if she had asked of him, he would have given her living water. What does he mean by living water? She is puzzled at his words, she questions him, how can he draw water when the well is deep, and he has no way to draw it. Jesus goes on to tell her that everyone who drinks that water will thirst again but the water he gives, they will never thirst again, it will become in them a spring of water welling up to eternal life. Is she puzzled still? What does this all mean? Is she going to give him a drink?

Not understanding the spiritual implication of his words it must have sounded like a plan to the carnal mind, she would not have to come to draw water ever again; then Jesus asks her to go bring her husband, why does he have to ask the dreaded question? That is the very question she has been trying to avoid answering. Reluctantly she replies, "I don't have a husband." Then Jesus begins to read her mail. She has had five husbands, the one she now has is not her husband. Now she perceives him to be a prophet since being a stranger he knows her life.

Strange Question

Something interesting is beginning to unfold here as she asks a question out of the blue about worship, what made her ask a question that is totally opposite of what they are talking about? What does worship have to do with anything? You would think she would be asking "how can it be that you know my past and the present having never met me?" No! She wanted to know where they are supposed to worship because her ancestors worshipped in a certain mountain and the Jews say it should be in Jerusalem where one should worship. Jesus tells her that the Samaritans worship what they do not know. Why did he make such a statement? Were they idol worshippers, having no idea what they worshipped? Maybe they were religious people who had no personal relationship with the Lord. Were they looking for God in all the wrong places? Jesus said, *God is a Spirit and they that worship him must worship him in spirit and in truth. (John 4:23-24 KJV)* She says when the Messiah comes, he will explain everything then Jesus reveals who he is, and the woman forgets what she came for, leaves her water pot and goes and tells everyone in town about this man.

Knowing who Jesus is, turned this woman into an evangelist. The whole city came out to see this man she was so excited about. Was there something different about her that made even the men of the city listen? Was her face radiant, and shining from having been in Jesus presence?

She had tried religion that did not work, she needed something more. Jesus was most likely the first man who was not looking to get something from her, who had shown her kindness, had not looked down upon her, who did not condemn her for the mistakes she had made. You can be assured this woman's life was never the same after that encounter with Jesus. When you have a real encounter with the Lord it does something to you, it changes you.

When Jesus comes into your life, he makes all the difference, you feel accepted, not condemned, loved and not used, forgiven and washed clean. Why did Jesus talk to the Samaritan woman? He was able to see beyond the outward appearance and get to the root of the problem. The real longing in her heart was not one relationship after another but her need for acceptance and fulfillment in her own heart. She needed a relationship with the living God and not the one presented by religion, which was the reason for her question about worship.

Most women are not looking for fulfillment in sex, relationships or drugs but acceptance as a person, needing to be loved without strings attached, loved for who they are and not what they can give. Jesus offers that love and accepts you just the way you are. When you give your heart to him you give him the most precious thing you have and it gives him something he can work with, he begins to bring out the person God created you to be, the one who has been hidden underneath the load of pain, guilt and shame.

You Are a Work in Progress

Total healing does not come overnight, nor are you transformed instantly but you are a work in progress and one day you will look in the mirror and not recognize the person looking back at you. The shackles will be gone, the burden will be lifted and looking back at you is this beautiful person God created, changed and transformed by the power of Almighty God. No, things are not going to change overnight but if you continue in the word, it will transform you. The Christian walk is a progression, step by step, day by day.

We are a work in progress, God is working in us continually, transforming our thinking and working with us until Christ is formed in us. God does not work by himself. We are workers together with him. None of us has arrived where we can say we have been perfected. We still have the human nature part of us which is being changed day by day.

There is a place in this relationship between God and you where you play a big part. There are many places in the bible where there are words like: say, be, let, put on or take off, the understood subject being you. God is not going to do for us what he has already done regardless of all our begging and crying. If he said you can do it, you can do it. The only thing that will stop you is you and your own insecurity due to the image of yourself that you have created.

God understands everything about you. He knows what motivates you to do the things you do; he even knows when you lie down or get up. You are not an impossibility that God needs to work with. You have not gone so far off the deep end that God has given up on you. There is no such thing as an impossible case with God. He specializes in making impossibilities possible and transforming lives. God never gives up on us, we are the ones who give up on God. We want answers to our prayers without anything being required of us and many times we pray without having knowledge of what already belongs to us

The woman at the well appeared to be an impossible case, a failure, looking for love in relationships, longing for change in her life but did not know how to make that change. Most people do not like the way they are, but do not know what to do to change their situation. The drug addict does not want to be the way he or she is, living from one fix to

29

another, losing his or her family, their self-respect, their reputation, living on the street. How does he or she get out of it? The homeless woman does not want to be the way she is, prostituting herself to get another fix, she just does not know the way out. Jesus sent us to go into all the world and preach the gospel to every creature. (*Mark 16:15 KJV*) We are supposed to tell them there is a way out of their situation. There is a better way to live.

Jesus came to heal all who are oppressed of the devil, to raise up those who have no strength to lift themselves up, to give rest to their souls. Jesus is amazing. He wants you free and he wants you to discover your true worth. Yes, he shows us our faults but never condemns. He always shows us the way out. He will never address your problem without giving you the solution and helping you make the needed adjustments.

CHAPTER 3

Woman thou art loosed

And behold there was a woman which had a spirit of infirmity eighteen years, and was bowed together, and could in no wise lift-up herself. And when Jesus saw her, he called her to him and said unto her, woman, thou art loosed from thine infirmity. And he laid his hands on her; and immediately she was made straight and glorified God, (Luke 13:11-13 KJV)

Have You Ever Felt Out of Control?

*D*O YOU CONSIDER yourself a free man or woman or are there things that are keeping you bound, things that keep you from becoming the person God created you to be? I once thought of myself as a free woman not realizing that I was still bound by regret, anger, fear, resentment and many other emotions. I felt anger inside of me, even angry at God because he did not rescue me when I needed him most. Have you ever been angry at

God? I was not a Christian at the time, so I cannot say I did it knowingly. I was angry at the world, angry at men and angry at myself. Anger was something I had lived with for so long that I made myself believe it was everyone else who had a problem, not me. Hurting people always want others to feel what they are feeling. One popular saying is, if they, if they did not act the way they did, if they would not say things I do not like, I would not be angry. Who are "they" anyway? I was quick to fly off the handle, I was not a nice person. Robert says I would get so angry I even kicked the cat. One day as he was coming home for lunch, he saw a stray cat fly out the door, he said he immediately lost his appetite and said, "I think I should stay away for now." I must say this though, after I kicked the cat, I noticed how skinny he felt, so I felt compassion for him and began to feed him and he became a fat beautiful cat. Sometimes bad things do turn out good even for cats.

Robert and I fought many battles in the earlier years of our marriage, he teases me now about how I would get physical and pull hair, now he is partially bald and says that is the reason why and I say that is because I won. I spent many nights sleeping on the seam of the mattress because I would not dare get near him. He could have all the cover and I would not ask him to share, I would rather freeze than share his cover. He liked to give me the silent treatment because he knew I hated it. I had pity parties no one came to. It is no fun when you spend unnecessary time feeling sorry for yourself. I found a way to get back at him though, I loved making noise when he was watching TV, like vacuuming or banging pots and pans. I do not suggest anyone do this, so do not try this at home, it may not go well with you.

I gave up on pity parties after they didn't work, I didn't get any satisfaction out of waiting to see if he'd come and say I'm sorry because it never happened, and a party is no fun without somebody to share it with. When you are angry you think crazy thoughts, like I do not care if he ever speaks to me again, I do not want to talk to him anyway. I did not like myself, I felt out of control. Thank God for Jesus and the Holy Spirit because I am no longer bound, I am now free from those crazy things I did. I have not arrived; God is still working on me.

Can You Relate to the Woman in the Bible?

Maybe you can relate to my bouts of anger, maybe you've experienced shame so that you feel intimidated, in the grip of regret unable to shake off the heavy burden of guilt and in the process you are making everyone's life miserable, not to mention your own life. You are not a hopeless case, there is hope for you. There was hope for me, you are not alone. I recall how hopeless I felt questioning whether I could ever change the way I was. Wondering what I could do to overcome the anger I felt. I hated myself because I could not seem to succeed at it no matter how hard I tried.

Many of the battles I was experiencing were those of my own making because of how I perceived myself. I know what it feels like wondering if people are going to find out about your past, wondering what are they going to think of you? I used to think, will it change the friendship, the relationship, their perception of me? Maybe it is better to hide under a mask and pretend you are someone you are not because it is too painful to face the truth, forgive and let go of what is making you miserable.

We must be real. If we continue to pretend that we are something we are not, we will live in misery.

Not knowing any better, I took the road that leads to destruction because of the lies that I believed. I was seeing myself as what other's termed "damaged goods" and because I believed the lies, I also believed that no one could love me. The devil is called the deceiver and rightfully so because he deceives so many into believing his lies. Let me assure you that God loves you and he understands you, He is touched with the feelings of our infirmities. (*Hebrews 2:18 KJV*) He understands you and your feelings like no one else can.

You must let go of the pain of the past because if you do not, it will come back and haunt you. How we see our self, determines whether we win or lose in life. Your destiny and your success depend on finding out who you are in Christ.

If we do not know who we are in Christ, it will control how we respond to others and will result in shyness and intimidation around other people.

For God has not given us the spirit of fear; but of power, and of love and of a sound mind. (2 Timothy 1:7 NKJV)

Timidity stems from our insecurity around others. The bible says fear has torment. (*1 John 4:18 KJV*) Fear can control the way we view things.

I remember when I finally broke down and shared with my husband the feelings I had held in for so long. We were on our way home from a Marriage seminar where my husband Robert and I were speakers. When we travel somewhere in the car we enjoy talking and preaching to one another. As we were discussing some of the questions the couples had asked and whether we had responded in a way that answered their questions, it opened the door for me to talk about the pain I had inside of me and the fear of rejection that I had experienced not knowing what my husband would think if I told him how my life had been affected by my past and the hurt and pain I carried for so long and about the innocent girl whose innocence had been stolen. Once innocence is taken, you can never get it back. I remember how we cried together because when you love someone you share the pain and the fears. We cried for that girl who had been taken advantage of and the innocence that was stolen.

I talked about the girl that blamed herself for not being able to change the situation. Once the hurt was brought out into the open something amazing happened, I felt the weight I had been carrying for so long just lift like a load off my shoulders. I felt as free as a butterfly who has just been released from its cocoon. It is always good to have someone we can confide in, someone who understands and can minister to our needs.

There is no amount of questioning, what if or if only, that cannot change anything, because you cannot go back and change what has been. You can only move forward.

Just as the woman Jesus loosed from her infirmity felt as she was made straight, that's how you will feel when you are willing to share the pain you've been carrying with the person you married or are about to marry even if it means running the risk of being rejected. Communication between couples is so important. It is through communication that we come to know and understand one another and how to live a peaceful life by avoiding strife in our marriage and in our home.

If you are a married woman, your husband married you because he loves you. If you never take risks in life you will never go far because fear will always hold you back. It is so true what the scripture says about fear having torment. FEAR spelled out spells false evidence appearing real.

It seems strange to me that in this age in which we live, where "anything goes;" women are still branded and judged by the world and they still feel used, abused and rejected. As I write this book many women are coming forward with the "me" movement, about the abuse they suffered in silence because of men who took advantage of them at the workplace or as they trained to become an athlete. I do not have any way of knowing how many of those accusations are accurate, but I believe many of them are true. I could have joined the "Me" movement, but I have chosen to join the "free" movement.

My question has always been why is it always the woman who is looked down upon? Why is the woman always made to feel unwanted and unloved while the man seems to be able to live a life of sin and never feel guilty about it or condemned, or do they? Do they also suffer in silence because they are supposed to be "macho men"? Society says men are not supposed to cry, if they show emotion, they are branded as weak. Knowing that we are all human and we all have feelings, I believe men also go through the same kind of things women do because I have known men who are broken over relationships that didn't work out and I know it affects the way they think and feel about themselves. They are just expected to react differently, to be the stronger one. Many turn to drugs and alcohol to deaden the pain. I know men who are troubled, bound and guilt ridden by abuse that took place when they were children. Young boys have been taken advantage of and they carry the guilt and the pain of it into their adult lives. They grow up confused about life and about their identity, God can heal the hurt and help them overcome the lies of the devil.

I say this about men because My husband Robert and myself once worked in a drug rehab center for men and some of the men that were brought to us had come out of broken homes, out of jail or out of drug rehabs that hadn't helped. Some were sexually abused and grew up confused about their sexuality. Our job description was to help them become free through the word of God. The men were with us for a year, in that time frame we were able to help some of them change through acknowledging what the bible says about them.

What About Women?

Religion teaches that women have no place in the church, women shouldn't teach or be in ministry, women should be quiet and learn from their husbands; the thing I couldn't understand about that concept was that many men wouldn't go to church if the wife didn't go and many women go to church without their husbands accompanying them, so where does that leave her? Does that mean that the woman cannot learn about God without her husband? Does it mean she cannot study or apply the word to her life? Many churches or religions today still operate under the law from which Jesus set them free.

I did not understand then, but I now know and understand that Jesus gave women a place they did not have under the law. The women who came to anoint Jesus body after his death were given the first message of the resurrection and were told to go and tell his disciples. It was the women who went to the tomb that morning while the men were cowering in fear in the upper room. It was the women who first saw Jesus after his resurrection. If women were to keep silent, shouldn't Jesus have known that? The scriptures about women keeping silent in the church and not usurping authority over the man, have been used to keep women from fulfilling the call on their life. (*1 Corinthians 14:34 KJV*) The woman is not to submit to all men, but to her husband and that in the Lord. In God there is neither male nor female as far as the gospel is concerned.

> *There is neither Jew nor Greek, there is neither bond nor free, there is neither male nor female: for ye are all one in Christ Jesus. (Galatians 3:28 KJV)*

Traditions of men have made the word of God of none effect and caused men to rule over women and children. Some cultures and religions of the world keep women under submission to men. In some cultures, women are stoned to death. It is so sad that in those countries the women are not allowed to even show their face in public. Thank God I live in America.

Human Trafficking

Human trafficking is a big trade in the day and age in which we live. According to Polaris, the International labor Organization estimates that there are 20.9 million victims of human trafficking globally. 68% of them are trapped in forced labor, 26% of them are children, and 55% are women and girls. My heart goes out to the victims of human trafficking. Lately we have seen children of all ages coming from other countries to this wonderful land of the free, where everyone can be someone, risking their very lives, and because of increase in human trafficking some are captured by evil people who abuse them and discard them as if their lives have no value. Every life counts. because every life was created by God. Many never reach the land of plenty, the land of dreams, the United States and those who make it often find it is not what they expected, yet manage to succeed because they come with determination to succeed regardless of what people say or the price they have to pay.

Human trafficking is a big business not only in other countries but right here in our nation, according to the internet, 2014 statistics show that 4.5 million people and increasing daily are trapped in forced sexual exploitation globally. I do not know what the statistics are today, I am sure they have grown since 2014. California has three of the highest child sex trafficking areas in the United States. I support some of the ministries that are rescuing many of these victims. I myself have not been involved personally in such a ministry. I admire those who have put their lives on the line to rescue children from the clutches of evil men and women who sell them into sexual exploitation and child labor.

Many young girls become involved in prostitution because poverty pushes them to do so. One in six runaway children is forced into sexual exploitation. Statistics show that most of the children that run away from home are between the ages of 12 to 14. Many young children trying to escape abuse or poverty do so in hopes of a better life only to find themselves jumping out of the frying pan into the fire.

If we do not minister to these people who will? Who is going to rescue them from the clutches of depraved evil people who take advantage of the weaker? Jesus ministered to all regardless of their circumstances. Aren't you glad that God did not require us to be perfect before he sent his son to die in our place, to set us free?

I have been to Central America and I have seen what poverty causes people to do for one meal a day; little adult children who never enjoy playing because they are forced to do their part to keep the family alive, young ladies getting up at 4 AM in the morning to walk miles to the city to sell their fruit and roots, then come home tired and discouraged with just enough money to buy beans and rice for an evening meal. I have personally met some of these young ladies. They are so humble and will generously invite you to share the little that they have.

The people of Central America are wonderful people with a heart of gold. The first time we went to Nicaragua for a minister's conference, I was so touched when the ministers took up an offering for us and I was reminded of the widow with two mites, she gave out of her poverty just as these people did. We did not want to take their money, we did not go expecting an offering but the minister we went with who was from Nicaragua told us to take it, it was an offering of love and acceptance, so we accepted it. I have learned to never say no to a blessing because it not only blesses you, but it creates a channel whereby they can also be blessed. Those ministers did not know us, they did not know anything about us, they did it out of honor for the ministry and out of a pure heart.

You are a Treasure Waiting to be Discovered

You are a treasure that has not yet been discovered. Countless beautiful people in our world today at one time were just like you, shrinking in shame, afraid of being exposed and rejected, afraid to let anyone know what their life had been. What made all the difference in them was they allowed Jesus to take their shame, their regrets and their guilt and uncover the beauty that was hidden beneath the layers of pain. God takes a broken life and continues to work with one so that as each painful memory is exposed, healing begins.

When gold is being refined it must go through a series of processes until all the impurities are removed and only pure gold remains. When we are born again, we become new creatures on the inside in our spirit, then we must go through a series of processes before we become the person God created us to be. As we study the word of God, we discover that many of our problems are a result of the way we think.

The importance of renewing your mind

It is so important to renew our minds because by nature we are drawn to the negative rather than the positive, before coming to the Lord, our thinking processes where formed by the way we were brought up and by the ideas of the world around us. It is necessary that we be transformed by the process of renewing our minds to think the way we are instructed to think according to the word of God. and to accept what God's word says about us. God is a positive God; he does not see negatives.

Our worst critique is ourselves. Who needs the devil when we are so good at putting ourselves down? We condemn ourselves and judge ourselves unworthy without any help from the enemy. We can discourage ourselves quicker than anyone else; why? Because we believe ourselves before we believe anyone else; no wonder we find ourselves bound by fear and concerned with what others may think.

We do not have to carry our cares, our fears, our shame, our pain because we were not created to bear burdens. The bible instructs us to cast all our cares upon the Lord because he cares for us. (*1 Peter 5:6,7 KJV*)

Why are Christians loaded down with the cares of this world? Because human nature says you must do something to help yourself, you cannot burden the Lord with all your cares, as if it is too much for him. It was Jesus who said, *come to me, all you who labor and are heavy laden, and I will give you rest.* (Matthew 11:28 *NKJV*) Cares cause one to concentrate on the problem and not on the one who can give one rest. It is when one's cares become bigger than ones God that we begin to lose hope. When hope is gone one loses the anchor to one's soul, the very thing that prevents us from being tossed to and fro and moved by the cares of this world.

I am reminded of a woman I will call Sue; Sue was a young woman sexually abused by her father. She came for counselling and prayer often but was never able to believe that God wanted her free or that he could show her how to be the woman He created her to be. She wanted to talk about it, but she was not willing to accept her freedom. I have found that people many times have become accustomed to carrying their cares, they really do not want to let go of them. They just want to talk about their problems. They want someone to listen, but they are not looking for a solution to their problems. They spend too much time dwelling on the past.

I had a Christian friend who has gone on to be with the Lord: but was never able to believe God could or would forgive her. We prayed with her countless times, but it did not produce results because she doubted that God would do it. One day she was diagnosed with cancer and given a death sentence. I visited her up to the day she passed, and I could never help her see the truth and believe, that Jesus had already paid the price for her sins. God had forgiven her since the first time she prayed but she was unable to accept her freedom because of her unbelief coupled with a guilty conscience. If a person's mind is not renewed by the word of God, one continues to listen to the lies of the enemy, and it is almost impossible to change the way one thinks.

The bible says it is through renewing our mind that we are being transformed. If there is no renewing of the mind, there cannot be transformation. For transformation to take place the word must be applied to one's life.

No More Safety Net

Maybe you have created a safety net to keep yourself from being hurt again. Jesus came to set you free to give you something to look forward to. Through the word you understand his love for you. He has already borne your sorrows and carried your pain so that you do not have to do it. (*Isaiah 53:5 KJV*)

Jesus, the Only Safety Net

I found that Jesus is the only safety net that protects us from the enemy. I am forever grateful that I came to know him. I was not only becoming calloused and unfeeling but angry and bitter because I had only known God through the dark lenses of religion. I did not know him as my heavenly Father who loved me, I did not feel worthy or deserving of his love. This was before I asked the Lord to save me, I had not even heard that I could do that, no one had ever shared with me the good news about salvation, which causes me to wonder how many other people have gone through life never having heard about Jesus. I would think that everybody would have heard about him because of the technology of today. When we went to Bacalar, Mexico and met many Mayans, it seemed like every young person had a cell phone. The young people who help in the ministry go into the remote villages to minister to people and invite children to their vacation bible school services. Some of the villages we went to are small villages with no running water or bathroom facilities. There were churches in almost every village because the people have become acquainted with the gospel through the children.

As I write this book, we are living under very unusual circumstances due to the Corona virus that has spread throughout the world and we are seeing protests and destruction on a scale we had not witnessed before. The pandemic caught us all by surprise, no one was expecting it. Jesus spoke about signs we would see before his return and the end of the age. We are witnessing things we had not witnessed in our lifetime and it causes me to wonder how people are making it without the hope we have in Christ. It causes me to ask myself the question, where would I be without the Lord? The bible tells us that hope is the anchor of the soul. Hope is what keeps your mind stayed on God and on the word. It keeps you steady in the storms of life.

God's love for humanity is not based on what we have done. We are not accepted by him because of our good works. The bible says that *we love him because he first loved us.*

(1John 4:19 KJV) We were lost in sin and while we were yet in that condition; he sent his Son Jesus to take our place, to pay the debt we owed and set us free. He did not wait for us to be righteous and holy before he demonstrated his love for us, we could not be righteous by our own works. Our own works could never be enough.

For by grace *are ye saved through faith and that not of yourselves; it is the gift of God; Not by works, lest any man should boast. (Ephesians 2:8-9 KJV)*

You might be reading this book because you like to read, and the title caught your attention or maybe someone gave it to you. It is not by coincidence that you are reading this book. The title caught your attention because you are feeling the effects of deep-seated pain that have spread forth roots of rebellion, rejection and anger and those roots have sprung up and caused feelings of helplessness, hopelessness and despair. Maybe you do not feel beautiful. Jesus is offering you the gift of his love; all that he asks of you is for you to take it, it is God's gift to you.

Some people reading this book have been to counselors and psychologists seeking help but leave feeling empty and without hope because only God understands what you are going through and why. Only God has the answers you are looking for.

All of us were born into this world separated from God because of Adam and Eve's disobedience which caused a separation between God and man, so each one is born with an emptiness inside that only God can fill. Man seeks to fill that emptiness with other things that can never satisfy. People have tried drugs, sex, fame and fortune to no avail because the spiritual hunger inside cannot be satisfied by natural means.

People tend to do things out of ignorance because of a lack of knowledge and lies which they believed, then find themselves caught up in an unending cycle of fear, rejection and relationships gone wrong.

Everything you ever want to know is in the Word of God; he has all the answers to everything. It takes lots of study of the word and applying it to our lives and situations to reach the place where the word becomes a part of us, and it begins to change the way we think. The word of God has been everything to me, my hope, my consolation, my freedom, my refuge, my strength, my safe dwelling place and my shelter from the storms of life. It is always there when I need it. I have never tried to memorize the word. As I read or hear it and act upon it, it gets down in my spirit and when I need it, the Holy Spirit brings it back to my remembrance. It is amazing to me how the Spirit of God brings an encouraging word to our remembrance just when we need it. The wisdom of God is in his word and it is there for the getting. The bible says, *Wisdom is the principal thing; therefore, get wisdom and in all your getting get understanding. (Proverbs 4:7 KJV)* We can have knowledge of many things but knowledge without knowing how to apply it is of little help.

In ministry I come across people who get born again and are on fire for God, but they don't realize that the initial feeling of utopia wears off and they must continue to study the word regardless of whether one feels God or not. Jesus said, *"if you continue in my word, then are ye my disciples indeed, and ye shall know the truth and the truth shall make you free."* (*John 8:31,32.* KJV) The word of God teaches you who you are in Christ so that you can begin to walk in the reality of it.

Problems do not fade away because we get born again, they increase because we soon find out that we have an enemy who does not want us to know what Jesus has done for us. The bible tells us that when the word of God is heard, the devil comes immediately to take the word that was sown out of one's heart. *(Mark 4:15 KJV)* We must guard our heart so that the enemy cannot steal the word that was sown.

There is nothing more liberating than understanding who you are in Christ and to know he has a plan for you that only you can fulfill because God created you unique. There is only one of you. You are one of a kind, children may look like you but each one has his or her own personality.

I tried so hard to be like other women but the harder I tried I still felt inferior. I never measured up because I was seeing myself through the dark glasses of the past and not through the Son-glasses of God's word. I was always too short; my clothes did not look exactly right; my hair was never as nice as others. I was afraid to talk because I did not think anyone was interested in what I had to say. I was shy and timid. Now I am confident in who I am because I have learned to see myself as God sees me and I have allowed the word of God to peel off those layers of insecurity, guilt and fear and discover the person God created me to be. It does not matter what others think because in the eyes of God you are beautiful, and He loves you.

> *I will praise you, for I am fearfully and wonderfully made; marvelous are your works, and that my soul knows very well. (Psalm 139:14 NKJV)*

You must see yourself as special in God's eyes as a beautiful woman with purpose. If we don't think we have purpose in life we live a "whatever will be, will be" kind of life, leaving everything to chance then one day we look back with regret because we lost out on so much and it's too late to recover some of the losses. We can always move forward and learn from our mistakes and allow the word of God to restore what the enemy has stolen. God is the one who gives beauty for ashes.

The Best Life Ever

I am not suggesting that the struggles of life will be over when you come to the Lord and choose to follow him, but I can tell you that you will not regret it. I never dreamed I would one day be teaching God's word, I never dreamed God would call me to the ministry or use me for his purpose.

Are you kidding? God using me, what could he possibly see in me? If anyone had told me I would one day be in ministry, I could not even imagine such a thing could ever be. Thank God he does not see as we see ourselves. The bible tells us that God looks on the heart and not on the outward appearance. he sees a heart that is pliable and easily molded, a heart that loves deeply and when loved back, loves without reserve. He sees a heart that is committed to the cause and will not turn back. I have determined in my heart to always have a heart that is open, teachable and subject to change, one God can work with, to follow him wherever he leads and to never allow anyone to rob me of the greatest treasure I have ever found.

Do you know that underneath the layers of the past lies a treasure that has never been discovered? Treasures are never found on the surface. Treasures are buried deep beneath the surface. God works with you as you openly admit your failures and weaknesses. The fear of rejection makes it difficult for one who has been abused to be able to admit their true feelings to others and let others come into their life.

What treasure could possibly be hidden underneath the ashes of your past? Is there a ministry waiting to be released, a song writer or possibly a singer, an author or a youth pastor? What treasure is hidden in you waiting to be discovered? What potential is waiting to be unleashed? Do you have a dream in your heart waiting to come into manifestation? Dreaming gives us hope. It gives us something to reach for, but we must believe that dreams can come into manifestation if we go after them to achieve them.

You are a diamond in the rough. God can take that diamond in the rough and fashion it into a light that reflects his image in you.

Today we hear people say they have issues and they use the issues in their lives as an excuse for their actions. A favorite saying of many is "I am the way I am, because I have issues that arise from being abused or neglected as a child." So many identify with the past which keeps one from believing there can be a brighter future awaiting them. I'm not denying the fact that things that took place in our childhood or any other time in our life can cause one to lose faith in people or cause one to do things they would have never thought of doing. Issues need to be brought out in the open and dealt with. We do not have issues, it is things we have refused to deal with, things that are too painful that we think by ignoring them they will go away. Pain never goes away by being ignored it must be acknowledged and we must be willing to forgive and let healing begin.

I look back on my own life and wish I had known the things I know now because it would have saved me from many years of pain, self-pity, resentment and anger and the struggles I experienced not knowing there was a better way or that I didn't have to live with the lies that I believed.

The wisdom of God is in his word; it teaches us how to become free and how to stay free. It shows us how to deal with our past and how to let it go. I understand it takes time for wounds to heal and many times it leaves scars that only love can erase. God loves you so much he sent his Son to take your place, to bear your pain and to set you free. There is no love you will ever experience like the love of God. His love is so precious and so wonderful. I wonder how I even survived without it. I suppose it was because He still loved me even while I was yet a sinner.

> *But God demonstrates His own love toward us, in that while we were still sinners, Christ died for us. (Romans 5:8 NKJV)*

It is so important that once we are born again that we study the word of God and learn how to be a doer of it, not only a hearer of the word but a doer, applying it to our daily lives.

> *But be doers of the word, and not hearers only, deceiving yourselves. (James 1:22 NKJV)*

We do not want to be forgetful hearers as those who say, "I've already heard that." My response to that is, if you have heard it what are you doing with it? God expects us to learn how to apply the word to every situation in our lives because the word of God contains the answer to every problem we will ever encounter in life.

Whenever I come upon a situation that I do not know how to solve; the word always has the answer for me. God always knows what our needs are before we ask.

There are two types of Christians, those who are called carnal Christians who never get into the word of God. They are satisfied with going to church and hearing a sermon, but never try to find out what is in the word for them, when things do not go their way they respond like an unbeliever. Then there are mature, spiritual Christians who have taken the word and applied it to their lives and see results. These are the ones who not only hear the word but are doers of it. A mature Christian knows how to respond in adverse circumstances, he knows where to find the answers in the word of God, and he knows how to make the word work for him. He stands firm in his faith because he has come to know God through the word and to believe that God is not a man that he should lie. All the promises of God are yes and amen.

One cannot have faith without knowing the author of one's faith. Jesus is the author and finisher of our faith. It is through faith that we receive the promises of God.

CHAPTER 4

What Do you Say?

ESUS WAS ASKED that question one day as he was in the temple teaching and suddenly there is a great commotion, the Scribes and Pharisees rush through the entrance of the temple bringing a woman and setting her in the midst where he was preaching. They say unto him, "Master, this woman was taken in adultery, in the very act, Now Moses in the law commanded us, that such should be stoned: but what sayeth thou?" (*John 8:4-5 KJV*)

To me that statement poses a few questions, where did they find the woman? Were they spying on her? How did they know it was the very act she was caught in? People who like to accuse others tend to be very graphic in their descriptions. Where was the man? The way I understand it, it takes a man and a woman to commit adultery. Why is it that the woman is accused of committing adultery, but the man is never mentioned? Where is the man anyway? Why didn't they bring him also? It is unbelievable that there are countries today where women are being stoned for committing adultery and the man continues in his adultery with no consequences for his sin. The bible says we can be sure our sin will find us out, nobody gets away with anything.

These Scribes and Pharisees are ready to stone this sinful woman. You can bet as they made their way to the temple, they scooped down picking up rocks along the way, ready to stone the woman. These are the religious leaders, the holier than thou bunch. They probably came in hopes that Jesus would agree to condemning the woman to death.

I love the way Jesus took control of the situation. He appeared to ignore them as he stooped down and wrote on the ground. Wouldn't we all like to know what he wrote? Some say he was writing the sins of her accusers; some say he was waiting on the wisdom of God before speaking. The bible says he never did anything without seeing his Father do it or say anything that he did not hear the Father say. I know he waited to hear what his Father would say.

What were the Scribes and Pharisees thinking when he stooped down to write on the ground? Did they think he was stalling for time? They were anxious to hear him say, stone her, they kept asking him, what do you say? They are getting a little nervous by now and agitated while they wait for an answer. Their hands are turning white clutching those stones, each one ready to cast the first stone, their attention focused on Jesus and what he would say.

The Scribes and Pharisees wanted the woman stoned, it is stated in their law that a woman caught in adultery should be stoned. My question is why the woman only? Lately I decided to read through the bible but when it came to the book of Leviticus, it is the hardest book to get through, but in Leviticus the bible says they both should be put to death. That was the law God gave to Moses to give to the children of Israel. Man is always quick to put his own interpretation to what the word really means. That is the way the devil operates. In the Garden of Eden, he said to Eve *"Has God indeed said, you shall not eat of every tree of the garden?"* (*Genesis 3*:1 *KJV*) The devil always tries to undermine the word of God. He wanted Eve to think God had not told them everything, that he was keeping secrets from them.

The men kept questioning Jesus until he lifted himself up, then they anxiously awaited his answer.

> *He that is without sin among you let him first cast a stone at her, and again he stooped down and wrote on the ground. They which heard it, being convicted by their own conscience, went out one by one, beginning at the eldest, even unto the last: and Jesus was left alone with the woman, he said unto her, Woman, where are thine accusers?* Hath no man condemned thee? *She said no man Lord, and Jesus said unto her neither do I condemn thee: go and sin no more.* (*John 8:1 to 11 KJV*)

The only one who had a right to condemn her was Jesus and he did not condemn her. We are so quick to pass judgement.

Aren't you glad that God looks on the heart and not on the outward appearance?

People have always been quick to pass judgement on others. The men were so ready to stone the woman caught in adultery, never taking into consideration that if there was not a man involved, she would not have been caught in the very act as they claimed.

In many countries, women have no education, they are not permitted to go to school, they have no skills, no means of supporting themselves and their families outside of prostitution.

The United States has always been known as the place of freedom and liberty for all, but it is not what it appears to be. Today our nation is changing rapidly. Young girls, boys and women are at the mercy of those who exploit them; it is nothing less than another form of slavery. The weaker being taken advantage of by the stronger. Righteous anger rises in me when I see the injustice in our world and the unnecessary suffering of humanity.

Jesus is seen time and again taking up for the weaker, that is my hero! He did not condemn the woman even though he was the only one who could have done it. I am sure the woman was shocked at the wisdom of the Lord. What was going through her mind as Jesus wrote on the ground? Was her life flashing before her eyes? Was she trembling in fear of being stoned? Was she wondering if Jesus was going to leave her at the mercy of her accusers? What a relief it must have been when the stones began dropping one thump, then another thump and another as the men began leaving one by one and she was left alone with Jesus. Was she still waiting in fear and trembling not knowing what the Lord would do? She must have been elated when Jesus asked; has no man condemned you? She must have been overwhelmed with relief when Jesus said, neither do I condemn you, go and sin no more. The Lord forgives us when we sin then he expects us to do as he told this woman, go and sin no more.

Where there is no personal relationship with the Lord, that person fears getting too close to him because he or she is not sure of what he will do. When we see Jesus in the scriptures as a faithful Lord of compassion, a Lord of love, one who lifts those who are cast down and heals the broken hearted one can draw near to him without reservation. He invites us to draw near to him.

> *Let us therefore come boldly to the throne room of grace that we may obtain mercy and find grace to help in a time of need. (Hebrews 4:16 KJV)*

What makes it possible for us to approach the throne of grace and draw near to God without fear? We can do it because he paid the price for our redemption, he has forgiven all of our sins and has made us the righteousness of God in Christ so that now we can approach the throne room and come expecting to receive mercy and grace for our time of need. We do not have to approach God with fear and trembling or begging him to help us, he said to come and obtain mercy and find grace in a time of need.

Any time you find yourself in need you can approach the throne room of grace without fear.

The Lord will never condemn you and you should never be afraid to draw near to him especially when you have fallen into sin. He is the only one who can lift you up and say those comforting words, neither do I condemn you, go and sin no more. When we sin, we should run to God not away from him

What a relief it is to know you are not condemned, knowing Jesus loves you and understands you.

Condemnation is of The Devil

The devil is the one who brings condemnation; Jesus did not come to condemn the world but to save it. The devil tempts you, and then condemns you when you fall into sin. If you are born again, you are in Christ and there is no condemnation if you walk after the spirit and not after the desires of the flesh.

> *There is therefore now no condemnation to those who are in Christ Jesus, who walk not after the flesh, but after the Spirit. For the law of the spirit of life in Christ Jesus hath made me free from the law of sin and death. (Romans 8:1-2 KJV)*

The woman caught in adultery lived under the law of sin and death. Jesus had not paid the price for sin yet; this was before the cross. It was written in their law that a woman caught in adultery should be stoned. Jesus was the only one who could save her because he had no sin. He rescued her from the clutches of the law and set her free by saying to her, neither do I condemn you, go and sin no more.

The Lord will do the same for you, he will take you out of the clutches of the enemy and show you a better way. He will erase the pain and the hurt and lift you up so that you can rise above it and find the peace your soul has been longing for. The only way you Can help someone else is to be free yourself. A treasure lies beneath the ashes of the past and God can take what the enemy meant for evil and turn it around for good.

Thoughts can torment especially when the devil is breathing down your neck accusing you and condemning you for what you have done. You must learn to love yourself, to see yourself as God sees you. Your identity is not in who you were but in who you are in Christ. Do not allow your past mistakes to identify who you are. You have made mistakes, I have made mistakes, who has not? Living in the past has never produced vision for the future. The mind being occupied with the past cannot imagine a future.

There's forgiveness in Jesus, you have not strayed so far that love cannot find you. When you surrender your life to the Lord, he will show you a better life, a better way.

We no longer live under the law as they did before Jesus paid the price for our sins. Today we live under another law, the law of the spirit of life in Christ Jesus. He made us free from the law of sin and death, free from the law that brought condemnation and death.

> *For the law of the Spirit of life in Christ Jesus*
> *hath made me free from the law of sin and death.*
> *(Romans 8:2 KJV)*

Today if we sin, we can run to Jesus in repentance and he will forgive us. As Christians we do not make it a practice to sin. Temptation to sin is present because of the weakness of the flesh. We commit sin when we enter in temptation and follow through. The bible says that God will make a way of escape in every temptation, but it is up to us to take it.

> *If we confess our sins, he is faithful and just to*
> *forgive us our sins, and to cleanse us from all*
> *unrighteousness. (1 John 1:9 KJV)*

God is a faithful God; he forgives us and cleanses us from all unrighteousness and puts us back in right standing with himself.

It is so beautiful how God takes a reject and makes him or her accepted, he takes a failure and makes him a success and he can take a broken heart and make it whole. He sheds his love in your heart so that you are capable of loving. For you to be capable of loving sincerely you must know God loves you, God heals, and God forgives.

I know it is hard to trust anyone when you have been hurt so many times or have known nothing but rejection and abuse. One can experience healing from ones hurts and pain because in Christ one no longer identifies with the past; but can experience a new life in Christ.

When suffering due to a broken relationship, abuse or neglect it is hard to trust a person that might abuse you and open the wounds that have not quite healed. It is like pouring salt into a wound. It is difficult to believe God can love you and accept you. It took several years for me to be able to accept the fact that Jesus loves me. I spent so many years rehashing the past that I was missing out on a better future. I allowed my past to dictate my future.

Your Identity is Found in Christ Alone

Your identity is not found in what or who you have been. Your identity is found in Christ alone. Only in him will you find your true value. You might find my book, *Stolen Identity*; helpful if you are struggling with your identity. I encourage you to get it and read it and let the Lord minister to you.

Why I Wrote Stolen Identity

I had no idea how to write a book or where to begin but when I obeyed, the Lord began to inspire me as to what to write about. I was able to understand how the devil stole man's identity in the Garden of Eden by enticing the woman to believe that God had left something lacking in their lives and that knowledge was only going to come through her eating the fruit God had told them not to eat of. I can imagine how the woman began contemplating the devil's lie, seeing how innocent the fruit looked and that it looked delicious to eat and fruit to be desired. How could something that looks so good be bad and why would God command them not to eat of it if it were going to make them wise like God? The devil never paints the whole picture or tells you what the end results of listening to him will be. He never lets you know how it is going to affect your life. In Adam and Eve's case it affected the whole human race.

How many of us would have had different life stories if we had known that the devil is a liar and nothing more than a deceiver? How many days and nights would have been spared from hearing the voice of regret pounding in our ears and the tormenting thoughts going through one's mind? How many days and nights of self-torture could have been avoided? As I look back now that I have grown in the word of God, and know the things that I have found out from God's word it gives me a desire to want to help others find the peace that I have found.

We cannot change the past, but we can certainly change the outcome of our future. Just because your life was not perfect it does not mean things cannot change, regardless of how things appear, no one lives a perfect life because of the nature of man. That is why we must be born again as Jesus said in (*John 3:3 KJV*)

I was born and raised in Colorado and recently we went to minister in a church close to my hometown. I told the congregation; I left Colorado many years ago, a sinner and came back a saint. I left Colorado lost, I did not know the Lord, no one had ever told me about Jesus or that he loved me and died for my sins even though we believed in God, no one told me I did not have to live a life of regret, thinking I was not worthy of anything good. It took years to realize that the things I did were done out of ignorance. I did not know there was any other way. I marvel at how many years I lived without the Lord because no one ever told me there was another way.

> *Jesus said for us to go into all the world and preach the gospel to every creature, He who believes and is baptized will be saved; but he who does not believe will be condemned. (Mark 16:15-16 NKJV)*

There is a song by Mercy Me; Dear Younger me. That song speaks of how different life would have been if he had known then what he knows now. How different would your life have been if you had only known then what you know now?

I now live in Texas and have lived here for many years, I like the car sticker that says; I was not born in Texas, but I got here as fast as I could. It was Texas where I met the Lord and where I grew up spiritually, it has been Texas where the Lord has blessed my family exceedingly and where my husband and I were called into the ministry. I am ready to go wherever the Lord leads. I never allow myself to become attached to things. As of this writing we live in the nicest largest home we have ever owned. God has blessed us so much, but we are willing to let it all go for the gospels' sake. I have never allowed things to have a hold on me because I know where they came from and the Lord will never leave me nor forsake me. If he can bless me in Texas, he can bless me anywhere in the world where he desires to send me.

> *A man's life does not consist of the things that he possesses. (Luke 12:14 KJV)*

It's one thing to have possessions and another to let those things you possess to possess you.

God is so good! I am forever grateful to him for saving me and for giving me new life. He has taught me to love and to have compassion, where I was hardened by hurt and regret, he has taken out the stony heart and given me a heart after his own heart.

He will do the same for you. He will show you how to live a life that is pleasing to him and how to let go of the things that are behind and how to reach for those things he has prepared for you. He will teach you how to love without fear of rejection because he will never reject you and his love will never cease to be. And when you fail, he will be there waiting to lift you up and strengthen you until you overcome the temptations that come your way. God believes in you.

He knows the potential that is in you, he knows your gifts and he his plans for you and they are good plans.

> *For I know the thoughts that I think toward you, says the Lord, thoughts of peace and not of evil, to give you a future and a hope.* (Jeremiah *29:11* NKJV)

God's plans for us are always good.

CHAPTER 5

The Wilderness Journey

*T*HE CHILDREN OF Israel were in bondage in Egypt for 430 years. They had been beaten, ridiculed, scorned and treated as less than human. God heard the voice of their cries and sent Moses to Pharaoh to deliver them out of bondage. God did great signs and wonders in the land of Egypt until it wore Pharaoh down and he finally consented to let the people go.

Can you imagine the excitement when they were finally let go and on their way to the Promised land? But before long Pharaoh changed his mind just as he always had and pursued them to the Red Sea. The excitement began to wane when they were able to hear the message being passed down from the end of the line "Pharaoh's armies are coming" and the people panicked. The Red sea was before them, Pharaoh's armies behind! What were they going to do? If they went forward, they would drown and if not, Pharaoh would have them slaughtered. They found themselves between a rock and a hard place. The Lord said to Moses to lift his rod and stretch out his hand over the sea; and divide it so that the children of Israel could go through on dry ground through the midst of the sea. (*Exodus 14:16* KJV) When they obeyed the waters of the Red Sea mounted up on both sides so that the children of Israel went over on dry ground. Do you think maybe there was fear in the children of Israel when Moses told them to go forward? They saw the waters rise up into a heap on both sides, maybe they thought they would be risking their lives not knowing if those waters would come down while they were going through, and they would be caught in the middle, but what else could they do? When the Egyptians assayed to do the same, they were drowned.

The place of growth and transformation

The children of Israel had been freed from physical slavery, but their wilderness journey had just begun. The land God had promised to them was filled with unknowns. Here is where the negative mindsets the people had developed while in captivity were going to be exposed, all their wrong thinking and attitudes, their fears and doubts were going to rise to the surface, everything was going to be a new experience for them, but it was also going to be a place of growth and transformation as their negative mindsets were turned into ones of victory.

God did not bring them through the wilderness to destroy them, he brought them that way to develop them and change their mindset from slavery to one of freedom.

For 430 years they had been told what to do and how to do it, remember that they were beaten, ridiculed, mocked and treated as less than human. They were overlooked as those who have no value. The abuse caused them to have a low self-esteem and to fear the unknown.

We get excited when we first become acquainted with the Lord, thinking our problems are over but being born again is just the beginning of our wilderness journey to the Promised Land. To get to that place of total freedom we must grow up and learn to face life head-on regardless of how painful it may be. We must get rid of the old mindset of bondage and see ourselves set free. We must learn how to overcome the enemy who's only desire is to kill, steal and destroy.

In the wilderness the children of Israel were threading unchartered territory. They encountered tests and trials that slavery had not prepared them for. The food and water they brought with them was not going to last forever then what were they going to do? God wanted them to learn that he was their provider. He rained down manna from heaven and provided water from the rock. He led them by a cloud by day for shade and a fire by night for light and warmth. The bible says he took them that way to try them, to prove them to see what was in their hearts. (*Deuteronomy 8: 2* KJV) The journey could have been over in 11 days but time and time again they murmured and complained because of the way.

No, it is not easy being a Christian because we must change our mindset. There are things the bible teaches about obeying the word and acting upon it and how it builds character in us and causes us to be a person that can handle every situation so that we won't be crying out every time things don't go our way.

What Will Your Wilderness Journey Do for You?

Your journey through the wilderness is going to make you or break you. It is going to show up areas in your life of weakness and things you need to change or get rid of. It is going to show you how to get over the pain of what you have been through so that you can help others going through the same things you have gone through. You are not alone in your pain.

There are many going through what you have been through and worse. We sometimes get so caught up in our own pain that we forget there are others in worse situations. The good news is we have God on our side, and he is working everything out for our good. God expects us to comfort them who are going through difficult times with the same comfort that we were comforted with.

God wants to make something beautiful of your life. We seldom stop to think of how a pearl is made. It's the irritating sand or parasite that gets under the oyster's shell that helps form a pearl, as it irritates the oyster it uses a fluid as a defense mechanism to coat the irritant, layer upon layer of this coating is deposited until a beautiful pearl is formed. In the same way we as Christians grow and develop as we learn to handle the things which irritate us

It is difficult to learn to live free when you have only known bondage. Maybe you have not known physical bondage as the children of Israel did but you have been bound in your thoughts and your emotions. On our way to the promised land we come out of our bondage by changing our mindset to relearn things God's way

You should never let what happened in the past lead you down the road to destruction. All you are going to encounter there is more heartache. The bible says *there is a way which seems right to a man, but its end is the way of death.* (*Proverbs* 14:12. NKJV) Death here is not necessarily talking about physical death but death of dreams, death of friendships, and death of relationships and self-respect. Once you have lost your self-respect it is difficult to get it back because of the voices of condemnation that come to haunt you. If you do not respect yourself no one else will respect you.

As you make your journey through the wilderness you are going to have to face things about yourself that you've tried to keep hidden and when you bring them out in the open, it can be painful. It is like rubbing salt into a wound. You are going to have to admit your weaknesses and your failures to yourself and accept what God's word tells you to do to change things, because it is not until we acknowledge our problems and do what the word says that healing begins.

I have learned to change the things I can and to leave the things I cannot change alone, and I am learning to know the difference. Sometimes we get frustrated trying to change people or change the things we cannot change instead of concentrating our efforts on changing the things that we can. Many times, the things that need to be changed are on the inside of us, things like pride, wrong attitudes, being judgemental, unforgiving, angry and resentful

Thank God I had great teachers who taught me the importance of studying the word and applying it to every situation I encountered. The word of God is what set me free. I am so thankful and grateful for God's word and those instructors who taught me about faith. I know by experience what God's word can do and I encourage you to study the word and put it into practice and see what God will do for you.

> *Study to shew thyself approved unto God, a workman that needeth not to be ashamed, rightly dividing the word of truth. (2 Timothy 2:15 KJV)*

In order to rightly divide the word of truth, we must first have knowledge of the word which comes from studying and comparing scripture, and not taking it out of context. James said if any of you lack wisdom let him ask of God. (*James 1:5 KJV*) God gives to us wisdom and understanding of the word so we can apply it to our everyday lives.

Throughout the years of ministry, I come across many Christians who do not know how to respond to the tests and trials that come because they think that going to church is all that is needed to be a good Christian. Year after year they circle the same mountain as the children of Israel did and they keep fighting the same battles year after year. I instruct people to face their giants head on as David did and not to back down because of the size of their problem but to concentrate rather on the size of their God. If we take our focus from our self and focus on how great our God is, we will begin to see things differently.

God's Word is Your Strength

If we want to be strong in our walk with God, we must study the word to know how to stand up against the wiles of the devil and be able to overcome through the word of God and faith in God's grace. When we know the Lord through studying the word, we know that the enemy has been defeated and we have nothing to fear. We can do as David did and boldly run toward our giant knowing that through Christ, the victory is ours. I know to some it may seem too good to be true. I too thought that way until I got hold of the word and understood it. That's how it was for the children of Israel, God told them to go in and possess the land because he had given it to them, but when they saw the giants they saw themselves as grasshoppers and they allowed fear to keep them out of the promised land.

Many of us have blamed others for our failures and weaknesses. If they would have sympathized with me, if they had not treated me that way, if they would just leave me alone, it is their fault all this happened to me. I ask myself who are "they" anyway? Blaming others is a crutch we use as self-defense. We cannot change what has been, but we can change what will be.

The apostle Paul said, *this one thing I do, forgetting those things which are behind, and reaching forth unto those things which are before, I press toward the mark for the prize of the high calling of God in Christ Jesus. (Philippians 3:13-14 KJV)*

Wouldn't it be wonderful just having one thing to do? That one thing the apostle Paul is talking about is a major thing that will lead you into freedom. Do not rely on your past to get you to where you are going. God has a plan for you and for you to fulfill that plan you are going to have to let go of the past as if it did not exist. In God's eyes you are a new creature, you do not have a past. Begin to reach for those things which are before and begin to press toward the mark for the prize of the high calling of God. To press implies work on your part, because you are going to have to press through all the failures, the hurt and things you have been through to obtain the prize. That is where the grace of God comes in to help you overcome the pain of the past and help you move forward to your new life in Christ.

I have known women who want to be free but do not know how to overcome temptation. When the tests and trials of life come, they find it easier to go back to the old lifestyle than to fight the good fight of faith. One of the mistakes women often make is falling for the same lines and getting themselves into one relationship after another, then they allow the condemnation of the enemy to defeat them.

I have heard women ask the question; how can God love me? You do not know what I have done. He loved the woman at the well, he never condemned her even though she had had five husbands and was living with one that was not her husband. He loved the woman caught in adultery and defended her. Jesus ministered to these women because he was able to look beyond the outward appearance and see their need. God looks on the heart and God understands you better than you will ever understand yourself. God loves you unconditionally.

The devil will lie to you in hopes that you will believe God does not love you anymore. If he can get you to believe his lies then you will begin thinking, what is the use? Why even try? I have already blown it, and you begin to draw away from him or anyone who has a relationship with him. See, when you get around other believers it brings conviction and feelings of resentment and anger because deep inside, you want to be like them, and you envy them. You think why can't I be like her?

One of my instructors in Bible school said when you have done things in ignorance because you did not know any better, sin is not imputed to you. But it does not mean the devil is going to leave you alone. If he can convince you of how bad you are, he can continue harassing you, until you totally give up on God.

If you have been delivered from bondage does that mean you are free? It is one thing to be delivered from bondage and another to be free. The children of Israel were delivered out of Egypt, but they were not free. They had to deal with many issues they did not even know they had until adverse circumstances showed up, and then they wanted to go back to Egypt rather than face the giants. Yes, sometimes we feel the same way; it just seems easier to follow the crowd, easier to flow with the current than to go against it. The children of Israel were taken out of Egypt, but Egypt was not taken out of them.

> *And you hath he quickened, who were dead in trespasses and sins; Wherein in time past ye walked according to the course of this world, according to the prince of the power of the air, the spirit that now worketh in the children of disobedience: Among whom we all had our conversation in times past in the lusts of the flesh and of the mind; and were by nature the children of wrath, even as others. (Ephesians 2:1,3 KJV)*

It is worth so much more to go against the flow than to let the current take you wherever it will. Yes, it is more difficult going against the current but if we never go against it, we will never develop the strength to overcome the obstacles that stand in the way. I heard one minister say, any dead fish can float downstream, it takes a live fish to swim upstream. I think I would rather swim upstream, how about you?

The world we live in today says, if it feels good do it, you are not hurting anyone, not realizing that we are not only hurting ourselves, but we are also hurting those we love most. The things we do, not only affect us; they affect those we love and care about and future relationships. I once had that devil may care attitude when I thought my life was in ruins, I did not care about anything, I just followed the crowd like a sheep to the slaughter. That kind of attitude was ruining my life and was causing nothing but heartache. We do not have to wait for our circumstances to change before we work on our attitude. Changing our attitude is also a work in progress because our attitude must be worked on daily.

It is so amazing how God has taken the ashes of my life and how he has turned them into something beautiful. Life in Christ is one thing I would not trade for all the money in the world. Why didn't anybody tell me there was a better way? Maybe it was because I lied to myself and made myself believe everything was fine just the way it was while my heart was breaking, and my life was falling apart. I felt helpless and hopeless, I felt like Humpty Dumpty must have felt. None of the king's horses or king's men could put him back together again.

It took the King of Kings to put the scattered pieces of my life back together again. It has not been a bed of roses I've had my wilderness journeys just as every believer has, But I have learned to recognize the giants that show up and the obstacles the enemy throws in my path and I have learned how to get the victory over them.

Each year gets more and more exciting as I discover new things that God wants me to know and I feel privileged to be in the ministry helping others come to the knowledge of the truth and to become victors not victims.

Every day with Jesus has been a new adventure. I have learned to trust him and to stay in faith knowing he will come through for me. I had to learn to allow him, to show me where the blind spots were, that I could not see and to bring correction when I have needed it. I have had to renew my way of thinking and adapt myself to his way of thinking. His way is so much better, he knows the end from the beginning; I only know the beginning and must walk it out by faith.

Changing your way of thinking is the biggest challenge you will face in the wilderness. For years you have been reasoning things out and doing things your way or letting someone else think for you, just as the children of Israel did while they were in bondage. I found out my way was only leading to disaster, so I began the slow process of learning how to act and speak the right way, in so doing I have avoided many pitfalls the enemy had planned for me.

Yes, renewing your mind is a process many Christians avoid because change isn't easy and it takes time, but stay with it until the mind of Christ is formed in you, then you will begin to find wisdom for every situation that presents itself. I had to learn how to rightly divide the word of God. If the bible tells us to rightly divide the word of truth, then there must also be a wrong way it can be divided.

> *Study to show thyself approved unto God, a workman that needeth not to be ashamed, rightly dividing the word of truth. (2 Timothy 2:15 KJV)*

There is a right way and a wrong way to divide the word of truth. If we do not study to show ourselves approved unto God, we could easily assume we know what we are doing and be led astray by our own interpretation of the word and lead others astray.

Once you get the word of God down in your spirit, you have something the Holy Spirit can work with. When a situation arises, the word will rise-up in your spirit just as it did in Jesus when the devil tempted him in the wilderness. Jesus said, *it is written that man shall not live by bread alone but by every word of God.* God's word is the only thing that defeats the devil every time. (Luke 4:4 *KJV*)

I thought being born again meant I was going to have it easy, everything was so new and exciting until one day I found myself in a deserted place, where it felt like I had back slid. I found out what the silent years are all about, a time when the skies seem brass and you do not hear God. I was not prepared for the wilderness. Yes, I studied the word and prayed but my prayers were shallow because I did not really know the bible nor the God I was praying to. I read the word, but I did not understand much of it. The church I was going to did not teach me how to avoid pitfalls or how to think differently or how to apply the word of God to my life. As children we were taught that no one could understand the bible, it was only for the priest. I thought I would never be able to understand it because the priest spoke in Latin and no one was able to understand unless one could understand Latin.

Traditions, whether religious or handed down by family are hard to break; they are handed down from generation to generation and will continue until someone gets born again and their eyes are opened to the truth

Have You Encountered Any Giants on your Journey to the Promised Land?

God told the children of Israel that he would drive the giants out little by little.

> *By little and little I will drive them out from before thee, until thou be increased, and inherit the land. (Exodus 23:30 KJV)*

And so, it is in our lives, little by little we learn to slay the giants as we grow in knowledge and understanding of the word. Confronting our giants face to face is something we must do if we want to gain the victory over them. We cannot do like the children of Israel and allow the size of our problem to intimidate us. We must be aware of the great God that we serve. When we see how big our God is, those giants begin to look small.

I was going from day to day blindly thinking I had arrived until I encountered giants bigger than me as I made my way through the wilderness. I had thought being a Christian was always going to be a mountain top experience. Once in the wilderness, I had to depend on God and his word to see me through. I found I was not alone because his presence went with me just as it had gone before the children of Israel as they wondered in the wilderness. God never promised we would not have tests and trials in life, but he did promise to be with us and to send us a helper, the Holy Spirit to guide us.

Thank God for the preachers on television that helped me understand the word. Their messages were like fresh manna from heaven and water from the rock. I could now see a clear path to the Promised Land and the giants became smaller as my knowledge of God and my faith in God increased.

The children of Israel were accustomed to being told what to do and were not even allowed to think for themselves. They did not get to enter the Promised Land because they murmured and complained about everything, nothing could satisfy them. Every time they got into trouble they called upon God and he delivered them but each time they turned back to their same old ways. The bible says they tempted God in the wilderness, they not only tempted him, but they questioned his ability to provide for them. Isn't that what we do? So often we question whether God can or will provide for us. We forget that he gave up everything for us and that the word of God says, *If God did not spare his only son how will he not then give us all things freely to enjoy. (Romans 8:32 KJV)*

We have a better covenant than the Children Of Israel. We are children of God, our covenant is based upon better promises, theirs was not. Jesus had not yet come to deliver them from sin. They were living under the law and the law had strict rules and regulation they were expected to live by.

The children of Israel were accustomed to having everything provided for them in Egypt and had become accustomed to slavery, many times they wanted to turn back to Egypt instead of continuing their journey to the promised land. At least in Egypt they had onions and leeks, they grew tired of manna from heaven. There may be times you might want to quit too because of the way, that is when you must encourage yourself in the Lord and keep on going. God has a better plan for you even though at the time you may not be able to see it.

The only reason Christianity seems so hard to many Christians is because they do not understand it is a process of going from one degree of glory to another. Each time we overcome in one area it is not the end, there are many more obstacles to overcome. We are growing and changing all through life, but it always gets easier as we go, we are gaining wisdom and experience with each year that goes by. We are learning to handle situations without falling apart. We learn to depend on God for guidance instead of leaning to our own understanding. We learn that God's grace is enough for us, when we cannot, he can! It is all about trusting God and learning not to lean to our own understanding. While we're leaning on our own understanding, we will always want to reason things out and try to figure out how they are supposed to happen, God wants us to walk by faith and to trust him to work out the details. The bible says, the just shall live by faith. Without faith it is impossible to pleases God. (*Hebrews 11:6 KJV*)

CHAPTER 6

Are You a Mary or a Martha?

*A*CCORDING TO THE Gospel of (*Luke 10:38,41 KJV*) Jesus came to the village where a woman named Martha opened her home to him. Martha had a sister named Mary. While Martha was preparing a meal, Mary sat at the feet of Jesus listening to the word.

Martha became upset because she was doing all the work and Mary was not helping her, so she came to Jesus and asked, Lord, don't you care that my sister has left me alone to do the work by myself? Tell her to help me.

> *Jesus answered and said to her, Martha, Martha, you are worried about many things, but one thing is needed, and Mary has chosen that good part, which will not be taken away from her. (Luke 10:41 NKJV)*

Are you a Mary or a Martha? Are you busy and distracted with so many things that you do not have time to sit at Jesus feet and listen to his word? Maybe instead of communing with God, you are telling him all your problems as if he did not know them already. Which is more important, to be heard or to hear what God would say to you?

In our world of technology, we seem to find less and less time for the important things in life. People are spending too much time on Facebook looking at what friends post or posting pictures or commenting on things, venting their frustrations and by the time they know it time has flown by and they didn't get much done, but they found out what people were doing, what's bothering them, what they are eating or where they are going. I use face book to write encouraging messages to lift people's spirits up, but I do not do much anymore because I get tired of seeing the same posts day after day from the same people. I believe we should take advantage of every opportunity as a means of spreading the good news. I like to see good posts by ministers, but I am not interested with all the negative things people post. It's always easier to vent your frustration when you're not face to face with the person you are upset at.

Getting back to Mary and Martha, which are you? So much of our frustrations stem from the attitudes we have about ourselves, how we see ourselves and how we think other people see us. We sometimes have this mentality that others owe us something and if they are not paying up, we get upset and start thinking there must be something wrong with me, why am I being treated this way, why isn't anyone helping me, why doesn't anyone care? It is all about me and it all boils down to concern about oneself.

Martha was busy preparing a meal but there is more to it than meets the eye. Jesus said she was worried about many things. She had a lot on her mind and because of it she was quick to cast blame on someone else and to demand that the Lord tell Mary to help her. When we are frustrated, we begin to blame and make demands on other people.

It appeared that Mary was just sitting doing nothing but, in all actuality, she was doing the right thing. She was seated at Jesus feet listening to him and Jesus said she chose the one thing that is needful that will not be taken from her. Sometimes we just need to stop doing the things we are getting frustrated over and sit at Jesus feet for a while and let the peace of God come over us. If only one thing is needful and that is to sit at the feet of Jesus and hear him, that means that is where we are going to find the answers to everything we need.

Where Does Frustration Come From?

Frustration comes from trying to do things in our own strength without seeking the strength that comes from spending time at Jesus feet. When we prepare ourselves spiritually for the day, things go so much smoother and everything turns out well as we rest in him and let his peace leads us. If we are frustrated and upset everything seems to go wrong and there is no peace but when we have spent time with the Lord everything turns out well.

> *Do not fret or have anxiety about anything, but in every circumstance and in everything, by prayer and petition (definite requests), with thanksgiving, continue to make your wants known to God. (Philippians 4:6-8 Amplified Bible C Edition B)*

I know that some reading this book are thinking, you don't know what I'm going through, you don't know how frustrating it is to clean house, do laundry, take care of kids and everything else that's crying out for my attention. We all have 24 hours in a day. We all have things calling out for attention, but Jesus said only one thing is needful and Mary has chosen that one thing. I also have a husband, a ministry, I've raised kids, worked outside the home, done laundry, ironed, cooked and all the other things women do but I have learned how to manage my time and put first things first and the rest will take care of itself.

Prayer Changes Things

I have discovered that spending time in prayer and reading the word is the best way to start my day. You do not have to spend hours on your knees or with your face in the bible. I like to spend at least an hour in the morning before getting out of bed just talking to the Lord or worshipping him. When I get up in a hurry and do not make time to pray my day does not go well. Sometimes all it takes is one word from God that stands out just when you need it. Sometimes a few minutes with the Lord will set you up for a blessed day. The great thing about having a relationship with the Lord is that you can talk to him any time you want during your day. His ear is always open to your prayers. He is always ready to help you in every situation that you encounter. There is nothing you will encounter in your day that you and God cannot handle. It is when you are trying so hard to do things on your own that you become frustrated and angry.

I try to get up with a positive attitude about my day. Attitude is everything. Attitude either makes your day or makes it miserable. I have learned to do what the bible says in (*2 Corinthians 10: 4, 5* KJV) I have learned and am still learning how to take my thoughts captive when they do not agree with the word of God, when they are trying to disrupt my day and when thoughts are causing me to have a negative attitude. God has provided a way to overcome unhealthy thoughts and behaviors and gain self-control. It is a matter of learning to channel our thoughts in the right direction, to bring them captive to the obedience of Christ. Have you taken the time to consider the thoughts that are going through your head? Do you pay attention to every thought or are you selective in which thoughts you choose to entertain? According to the bible we can be transformed by the renewing of our mind. What does that mean? It means that we must learn to think in line with the word of God.

Meditate on the Healing not the Hurt

Depression, anger, and resentment come from the negative thoughts that we have. The natural mind likes to hang on to past offenses, like a video, it will play them over and over in your head, which results in you feeling angry and wanting to defend yourself and hurt the person that hurt you. Did that person really hurt you or were you hurt by how you perceived things and the amount of time you allowed yourself to meditate on the hurt instead of the healing? Life is simple, but people insist on making it complicated.

The first thing we must do is take responsibility for our thoughts. You can control what you think. The apostle Paul said we should think on things that are true, lovely, honest, and of a good report, things that are pure. We must replace bad thoughts with good ones. When we think wrong thoughts, we begin to worry about things that may not be real, things that produce fear, things that rob us of our peace. What we think on has a lot to do with how we perceive things. You might think everyone is better than you, but you only see the image they portray to others, you do not know what is going on inside the person. We all have our own fears and weaknesses. When we compare ourselves to others, we always come up short.

We do not forgive a person because they deserve it, we forgive because we deserve peace. Being angry at someone who hurt you, hurts you more than it hurts the one you are angry at. When we forgive it means we can let it go and go on with life. When you forgive, you are setting a prisoner free and that prisoner is you.

You must take the limits off your life. If you do not take risks in life you will never know what you can accomplish. You will never reach your full potential wishing and hoping. It is in doing that things get done. Do you have a dream in your heart? Is there something you hope to accomplish in your lifetime? What drives you? What do you enjoy doing?

You must learn to be a master rather than a servant of your thoughts. The Bible says you must take every thought captive if it is exalting itself against the knowledge of God. Your thoughts are not supposed to take you captive. You are the one who should take every thought captive that causes you to feel bad or sad or angry. You must not allow others or circumstances to dictate how you think or feel.

> *For though we walk in the flesh, we do not war after the flesh: For the weapons of our warfare are not carnal, but mighty through God to the pulling down of strongholds; Casting down imaginations, and every high thing that exalteth itself against the knowledge of God, and bringing into captivity every thought to the obedience of Christ. (2 Corinthians 10:3,4,5 KJV)*

So much of our frustrations come from trying to change others instead of focusing on changing ourselves. We are never going to succeed at changing someone else. We were never meant to change others but to change our self and amazingly others will change. Many times, we find that when we change our way of thinking and it changes how we respond then the other person is not such a big problem as we assumed. Try thinking on what you do have rather than what you do not have. The way you think determines how you feel about yourself and others. Some call it stinking thinking. The Bible says for *as he thinks in his heart so is he*: *(Proverbs 23:7 NKJV)* That's why we must examine the way we think to determine if some of our problems are being produced from the way we see our self. That is why it is so important to see ourselves as God sees us.

The reflection in the mirror

What do you see when you look in a mirror? Do you see your imperfections and blemishes and what you want to change? When we look in God's word, we see a reflection of who we really are, of how God sees us, but we must believe that it is possible for us to become that image God has of us. God sees you beautiful, a child of the living God, created in his image. He sees talent and potential in you that you cannot see because you have been blinded by the poor self-image you have portrayed of yourself.

I was so shy, almost afraid of my own shadow. I had an extremely poor self-image. I saw myself through the eyes of my past. All of that changed when I began to look in the word of God and was finally able to let go of the past and began to see myself as God sees me. I want to be a confident woman who is bold and stands for what she believes. I no longer allow those ghosts of the past to haunt me because I have a new life and I have purpose and I am important to God's work and his kingdom. There are no more skeletons in my closet. God helped me clean up my closet and helped me get rid of skeletons of failure, fear and regret that popped up every time I opened the closet door.

Get Rid of the Skeletons

Get rid of the skeletons in your closet. You will find when you get rid of the skeletons of the past the ghosts of past failures will disappear. How do I get rid of the skeletons of my past? The word of God contains the answers to all your questions. As you read and study the word you will begin to see yourself as God sees you and as you become acquainted with the word and the Holy Spirit begins to reveal it to you, you will come to have faith in what the bible says about you.

CHAPTER 7

Will he find faith on the earth?

JESUS SPOKE A parable in (*Luke 18:1to 5 KJV*) about a persistent widow woman who would not take no for an answer. This woman was a widow who knew her rights. The parable says that there was an unjust judge in this city. This judge did not fear God and he did not care what people thought. He lacked compassion and mercy. The woman came to him and requested that he avenge her of her adversaries. The judge refused but the woman was persistent. She did not give up. The bible does not say that she kept making this request daily, it does mention what the unjust judge said. He said he did not fear God or regard man but because of her continual coming she bothered him, so he gave her what she requested. I like to get into the story, so I see this woman's presence every time he came to the office, maybe she said something maybe she did not say anything, nevertheless her presence made him uncomfortable. Later in the parable, Jesus said *when the*

Son of man comes will he find faith on the earth. (Luke 18:8 KJV) Jesus is talking about the kind of faith that does not quit, does not give up. Faith that does not consider the circumstances. Faith that gets results.

How much does it mean to you to be avenged of those who have hurt you? Have you persistently sought relief without finding it? God is not like this unjust judge; He is a merciful Father who wants the best for his children. He sent his Son Jesus to take our place and our punishment so that we do not have to live in bondage. It is not a question of will he avenge you? It is a matter of how much you want it and how long are you willing to wait and stand in faith believing.

What Kind of Faith do You Have?

God has given to each one the measure of faith, but it is up to us to build it up. We can have no faith, little faith, shipwrecked faith, strong faith or faith that will not take no for an answer. What kind of faith do you have?

> *So then faith cometh by hearing, and hearing by the word of God.* (Romans 10:17 KJV) It does not come from having heard, rather from hearing and hearing until it becomes revelation to your spirit. Once it becomes a revelation no one can take it from you, it has become your revelation and you can trust that when applied to your life and your situations it will work for you every time.

Some people get angry because they see others succeed and they are thinking, I go to church, I tithe, I am a good person, then they ask, why isn't God blessing me? God does not bless us based on our good behavior. God blesses us according to the knowledge and revelation we have of his word. When you hear a message, that message must become yours. There is a big difference between hearing the word and doing something with what you hear.

Many Christians have weak faith because they are led by what they see with their eyes, what they hear and what they feel. That is what causes one to have shipwrecked faith. It is our five physical senses that many times contradict the word of God. We are accustomed to basing our conclusion on what we see, what we feel, what we hear, what we touch and what we smell. That is the carnal nature of man. When you get born again you take on the nature of God in your spirit. You are a three part being, you have a soul, you live in a body, but you are a spirit. God speaks to you through your spirit. Your spirit is alive unto God, but your soul and body are still governed by the five physical senses and that is the reason why the bible says we are to be transformed by the renewing of our mind.

The only safe place

We live in an age where evil is all around us, the thoughts and imaginations of man's heart are evil continually just as it was when God told Noah to build the ark. The only safe place is God. He is our safe dwelling place, our refuge from the storms of life, but you must believe the word. Jesus prayed that God would keep us from the evil one. (*John 17:15 KJV*) When we make God our habitation according to God's word, *no evil shall befall us, and no plague shall come neigh our dwelling. (Psalm 91:9,10 KJV)* Faith comes by the hearing of the word and faith's foundation is built on knowing God and knowing the word of God. If we want to have strong faith, the kind that is persistent, we must hear the word and then be doers of the word and not hearers only. The bible tells us that when we hear only, we deceive ourselves.

We have an enemy, the devil. Many people think he is someone with horns and a tail and a red suit, but the devil is real. He is spoken of in the bible. He tried to get Jesus to do what he wanted but Jesus spoke the word against him, and he left.

Many believe the disasters and tragedies we are seeing today are acts of God. Insurance companies call it an act of God. The bible makes it clear that Jesus came to give life not to take it. The devil is the thief who comes to kill, steal and to destroy.

When Adam and Eve disobeyed God in the garden of Eden, they turned over their authority to the devil, but God through Jesus victory over Satan has restored our authority. The only authority the devil has now is what you and I give him. That is why it is so important to know what the bible says about the devil.

> *We are not ignorant of his devices.* (2 Corinthians
> 2:11 KJV)

The enemy does not want you to know you can be set free. He wants to keep you in bondage because that way he can keep you from being the person God created you to be. If you believe you are unworthy and of no value, he can keep you from succeeding in life. God wants you to succeed. He has placed in you gifts and talents that are being wasted. Those are the hidden treasures within you that he wants to bring out.

A couple of years ago, and happening as I write, there have been and are numerous fires and landslides in the state of California and a few days later neighbors of those who lost their homes began to dig through the ashes for treasures that had personal meaning to those who lost their homes. That is what the word of God does for you, it finds the beauty in the ashes of your life. The word of God says you can do it. God believes in you, believe in yourself and believe that God can turn your ashes into beauty. Let go of that failure mentality and believe that God has great things in store for you.

You are not in this alone. There are many who are in bondage by the chains and shackles of the past. They do not know there is a way out. They do not know or believe that their life can have meaning. Jesus is the way out. He will set you free, once you are free you can make a difference in other people's lives. You can help them reach their potential. When you encourage people and communicate with them on an emotional level, it creates a bridge between you and them. It builds up their confidence and a sense of self-worth.

If you continue in my word, then shall ye be my disciple indeed and you shall know the truth and the truth shall make you free. (John 8:31 KJV)

I am a living testimony of what God's word can do. I have been bound and now I am free and free is a million times better. Freedom gives you peace that goes far beyond your understanding. Freedom gives you the confidence you need to feel secure and confident in yourself and to believe you are loved by God and he has plans for you.

Becoming a Confident Woman

Do you want to become a confident woman? Do you want to be bold, confident and sure of yourself? Does being confident depend on how you look, your shape, your personality or what others think of you? The word of God is what gives you confidence to lift your head up high, to believe you are special because you are a child of God. In God's word you see the real you, the person God created you to be, a true reflection of how God sees you regardless of how you have been seeing yourself. You are a new creature in Christ, you are redeemed, you are the righteousness of God in Christ Jesus. You have been bought with a price, the blood of Jesus, you are worth so much more than you can ever imagine. God gave his only begotten Son to die for your sin and to give you a new life. You are precious in God's sight.

Your position in Christ does not change because you miss it sometimes and fall into temptation, his love is not based on your performance. God believes in you even when you cannot believe in yourself. When you miss it, pick yourself up and keep on going, do not allow your faults to defeat you.

Quit comparing yourselves to others, quit looking to see how well they look or seeing their faults. When we look at the faults of others for some reason it makes us feel better about our self because it makes our faults seem less than theirs. A prideful person will see the faults in the other person and elevate their self. If you are a humble person, it ends in you deflating yourself because you do not measure up. Do not put your confidence in man, man will fail you, God never will.

How do I become a confident woman? Develop self-respect, quit concentrating on the past and begin to look, into the mirror of God's word. Develop self-esteem, see yourself as God sees you. God sees potential you cannot see. Believe in yourself.

Learning to Trust God

I had to learn how to trust God due to all the insecurities I felt I found it hard to believe it was possible that I could be free. It was in studying the word of God that I found that I did not have to be a victim of my circumstances but that I could have victory over them. The reason I talk so much about studying God's word is because it set me free and it will do the same for you. For many years, my life was ruled by the victim mentality I had of myself, a "poor me" mentality. I changed my mindset from victim to victor, to that of an overcomer. I was able to triumph over my circumstances and become victorious, not through my ability but by his grace. God will give you grace to overcome and grace to help when you feel weak.

The Lord wants to help you become an overcomer. He wants to show you what it is like to be free. He has chosen you to succeed. He chose you because he loves you and his plans for you are bigger than you can imagine.

There was a time in my life I did not think I could accomplish anything. I did not think I had any talents or anything God could use. Today I am a teacher of the word which I love and enjoy more than anything. I am a writer, an inventor, a floral designer, I love to decorate, and I love music and singing.

Next time you look in the mirror, tell yourself you are loved by God, that you are an overcomer, that you are beautiful, and you have worth and purpose because the King of kings has chosen you. Say what the bible says about you in (*Ephesians* 1 *KJV*) The bible says that you are loved, accepted in the beloved, adopted and have an inheritance in Christ.

Faith becomes a lifestyle for the believer. Faith is sometimes called the sixth sense because faith does not respond to what the five senses respond to. Faith responds to the word of God.

The bible says you are precious in God's eyes. God created you in his image. You are wonderfully and fearfully made. The bible compares the word of God to looking in a mirror. When you look in the mirror of the word you do not see imperfections or failure as you do when looking into a natural mirror, you see what God sees.

Faith is Now

> *Now faith is the substance of things hoped for, the*
> *evidence of things not seen. (Hebrews11:1 KJV)*

Faith is believing even when there is no physical evidence. According to the bible Faith is now, not tomorrow because tomorrow always puts faith in the future. While we keep faith in the future instead of now it cannot work for us. Faith is believing even when we cannot see it. Faith is the evidence that what we are believing for is there and faith gives it the substance needed for it to become a reality.

We saw earlier where Jesus asked the question, when the son of man comes, will he find faith on the earth? He is not talking about finding natural faith that we all have but faith in what we cannot see, feel or touch. The widow woman stood her ground even when she was denied her request. She didn't take no for an answer, she didn't say "que sera, sera," I guess that's just the way it's got to be." She continued to make an appearance until she wore down the unjust judge's resistance.

How long are you willing to stand your ground against the enemy who constantly bombards your mind with negative thoughts? When are you going to begin resisting the lies of the enemy and say this is where the buck stops? God has already done what he is going to do, now it is up to you to let your faith do the talking instead of your circumstances. Which is speaking louder, your circumstances or your faith?

Faith has a Voice

The bible says faith speaks; faith has a voice. (*Romans 10:6-12 KJV*) It is your faith you want the enemy to hear. If you are allowing your circumstances to dictate what you say, you are defeating yourself with your words and not allowing God to work on your behalf.

The most difficult thing for any Christian is learning to speak what you want and not what you see. I recall the first time we heard that we must train ourselves to speak positive instead of negative, it was so hard. It is difficult for those of us who were not raised in church or taught the word of God to change what we are accustomed to, to what is written in the word. We made it a family project, every time one of us would say something negative, the others would say, it is your confession and I believe it will come to pass. The bible says you can have what you say if you believe and do not doubt. (*Mark 11:23 KJV*) We began to change our words from negative to positive.

God is a Faith God

God is a faith God; he calls the things that be not as though they were. (Romans 4:*17 KJV*) We must train ourselves to speak what we want and not what we see or what we have. Poverty for example concentrates on the lack, on what it does not have, on what it cannot afford. Sick folks concentrate on their feelings, on the symptoms and on the pain. Faith is the substance that brings the thing we hope for into existence.

Fear on the other hand has a negative effect. Fear will make void what you are believing for. Faith and fear cannot be in the same place at the same time because one will make the other ineffective. We have trouble understanding faith because we want to understand it from a human perspective. Faith is understood by the word of God, believing what the bible says and acting upon it.

Everything we do in life is done by faith either natural or spiritual faith, or faith based on the word of God. In the kingdom of God, the just shall live by faith, it becomes a lifestyle to the believer based on the word of God. If you can find it in the word, you can apply it to your situation by faith and God will look after his word to perform it.

Most Christians have no trouble believing that God will do it, they have trouble believing that God will do it for them. If you are trusting God to help you overcome things in the past, you must first know God, believe his word and then apply it to whatever it is you need him to help you with.

Words are a Creative Force

Start by saying what God's word says about your situation, meditate on it until it becomes a reality in your life. God put creative power into his word, when you speak it, it will create what it says if you do not mix what you say with negative words. All words have creative power either for good or for bad.

> *Death and life are in the power of the tongue;*
> *and they that love it shall eat the fruit thereof.*
> *(Proverbs 18:21 KJV)*

You have the power to create life or death to a situation by the words you speak. The word of God teaches us to speak positive instead of negative and to be careful what we say.

I know many think it is too far-fetched to believe, but God said in his word that words create life or death and those that love it will eat the fruit thereof. In the 1980's there was a lot of error in confessing the word because many Christians thought they could confess anything they wanted, and it would come to pass and the Christians who believe the word of God were called the name it and claim it bunch.

Jesus taught us the importance of the word of God, but he never said for us to name it and claim it, he said to say it and believe it and do not doubt in your heart.

> *For assuredly I say to you, whoever says to this mountain, be removed and be cast into the sea, and does not doubt in his heart, but believes that those things he says will be done, he will have whatever he says (Mark 11:23 NKJV)*

The principal here is to believe and do not doubt. We are accustomed to speaking negative, so it seems strange to us to speak positive about our situations. We do not have any problem talking about our problems and repeating how bad things are over and over, but we think it strange to speak positive about our situation and speak the word over them.

If we want to see success in our life, we must do what the word of God says and refuse to doubt regardless of how the circumstances look in the natural. I realize that we all go through things in life that seem impossible but then we look back and realize God was there all the time, working everything out for our good. We serve a wonderful God.

CHAPTER 8

God has a plan for your Life

For I know the thoughts that I think toward you, saith the Lord, thoughts of peace and not of evil, to give you an expected end. (Jeremiah 29:11 KJV)

GOD HAS GOOD things planned for you because he wants you to succeed in life. He has made you the head and not the tail. He has taken you from where you were to where you are now because he wants to show you how wonderful life can be when you surrender to his plan.

We can plan our own way, but success is not guaranteed when we make our own plans as to what we think God has for us. Even as Christians we fail because we want to do things our way, not taking into consideration that God's ways are so much higher than our ways. It is human nature to want what we think is right for us. But God has ways that are so much higher than our ways. God sees what we cannot see.

> *For my thoughts are not your thoughts, neither are your ways my ways, saith the Lord. For as the heavens are higher than the earth, so are my ways higher than your ways, and my thoughts than your thoughts. (Isaiah 55:8,9 KJV)*

How Do I Find God's will for me?

I had a struggle in my own life at times because I knew God's general plan for me, but I did not know his specific plan for my life. I knew he called me to teach and there is nothing that gives me more pleasure than teaching his word. I love to dig into the word of God, and I love it when the Holy Spirit reveals truth to me that I can teach to others. I am totally dependent upon the Holy Spirit. He is my best friend. At times I have tried to do a message on my own, but it always falls flat, and I recognize my need for the Holy Spirit to direct what I teach others. Even in writing a book, I will check it over and over and make changes as I feel led to do so. I am a perfectionist and I like to do things right, but I am not an English professor, so I must be careful to word things in a way I believe it benefits the reader.

As I said earlier, we are presently in a time of transition. We have been pastors for the last 17 1/2 years and now we are entering a new phase of our ministry and it is hard for me at this time because there have been so many changes take place in 2020 and we are sort of at a standstill because we are seeking God's specific direction for this season of our life. This is where I must trust that God knows best. I think of Moses and how he knew God wanted him to deliver his people from slavery and went about it on his own and had to flee to the back side of the desert where he spent forty years waiting to get God's plan. I do not want to spend the rest of my life on the back side of the desert where the silence is so loud that I feel like somehow God has forgotten me.

Jesus was led into the wilderness forty days and forty nights before he began his ministry. After having fasted forty days and night he was physically weak, and the enemy came immediately to tempt him. The devil did not know that having fasted and spent time in the presence of God had made Jesus spiritually strong and well able to resist temptation with the word of God.

Have you ever had those silent years when it seems like God is not communicating with you, he is not answering, or seems distant? I have had some of those, where it seems like God is silent and you so want him to speak, to say something, anything, but there's only silence. I believe that's when God wants us to consider just how much we really want what we are asking for. What are we willing to give up in order to follow him? They say silence is golden but not when God is silent. In my life it is at those times that I take inventory of my life and I am learning to follow the Holy Spirit's promptings about things I need to change or take care of in my life. I believe it is part of our preparation because of what lies ahead. No one runs into the plan of God by accident or has God's plan laid out for him from start to finish. We must walk it out one step at a time because it takes time to grow and mature in the things of God. We must be well prepared for the task he has for us, so he takes time to prepare us for it. Much of our walk with God is done by faith, trusting and believing that if God calls us to a special task, he will see to it that we are well prepared for it especially in these times in which we live.

Many who have stepped out ahead of God have failed not waiting for his plan. When we get out of the will of God it hurts people and God is not pleased when his people are hurt by our foolishness.

In the year of 1988, a minister gave us a prophetic word about how the preparation for our ministry was going to be long because of the work God had for us to do. At that time, we were thinking ten years, it has now been 30 years and we are just beginning to step into that phase of ministry. God's timing and ours are totally different.

Sometimes people get a word from the Lord and think it's supposed to happen immediately and when it doesn't happen, they try to make it happen and end up discouraged and frustrated, sometimes giving up on God and ministry.

God told Abraham he was going to be the father of many nations. Sarah his wife was barren, so it seemed like an impossibility, so Sarah figured since she was barren, she would suggest Abraham have a child by her maid. (*Genesis 16:2 KJV*) Abraham did not think it was a bad idea, but it was not the promised child and they began to have trouble. When we do not wait on God, we do things in our own strength that produce some results but not the results God has planned for us and it ends up hurting not only ourselves, but others as well.

> *But they that wait upon the Lord shall renew their strength; they shall mount up with wings as eagles; they shall run and not be weary; they shall walk, and not faint (Isaiah 40:31 KJV)*

Wait for what? Wait for His direction, his plan because when you have his direction and his plan you can mount up on wings as eagles and you will run and not be weary of the journey and you will walk and not faint.

As we wait upon the Lord, he increases our strength and our patience and furnishes the ability so we can mount up with wings as eagles. Eagles see a storm approaching, they have the power to soar above the storm and so it is with us as we wait upon the Lord it gives us the ability to soar above the storms of life. Waiting upon the Lord strengthens us, so that we can run without growing weary. So many of us grow weary of the journey and many times think about quitting but we are not quitters, we must learn to walk before we are able to run.

There are times when we can take a thing and run with it, then there are times when we must walk things out and in time we learn when we are to walk and when we are to run. Many times, we grow impatient while waiting. God is trying to teach us to wait, to let patience have her perfect work that we may be entire lacking nothing,

> *But let patience have her perfect work, that we may be perfect and entire, wanting nothing. (James 1:4 KJV)*

Maybe you are thinking, I do not know if God has a plan for my life, I have messed up so many times, I do not know if he can use me. God is in the business of restoring lives. He is always ready with open arms to receive you when you come to him in repentance and are ready for change in your life. God never refuses anyone who comes to him, even the worst sinner is received. God delights in helping people change.

God's plan for your life begins through a personal relationship with the Lord and the study of the word, it's in the word of God where you are going to find out what pleases God and what you must change in your life to become a vessel of honor that he can use for his glory.

In studying the word, we begin to understand how God leads us and what his will is. Just before Jesus went to the cross, he talked to his disciples saying that he would send them another comforter who would not only be with them but would live in them and this comforter would lead them into all truth. He told them he would send the Holy Spirit to them. (*John 14:16 KJV*) The Holy Spirit is our guide or our tour guide. He knows the paths and the trails we are supposed to walk in, and he can direct us into the perfect will of God. Many times, in our attempts to follow the Holy Spirit we take a detour off the path where he is leading, and we encounter heartache, discouragement and disappointments.

Maybe you are not called to a pulpit ministry or public speaking but there are many other areas called the ministry of helps. There is a place where you fit in. You will discover through volunteering in your local church you will find your place; it will be where you function best, and you have peace in your heart. Many people are called to a supportive role where they help finance the preaching of the gospel. You can be just as much of a blessing financing the gospel as those doing the ministry. God blesses ministries through generous giving people and then turns around and blesses them more, so they can be a greater blessing.

What is in your heart?

What is tugging at your heart strings? When I got born again my first desire was to know God and to find out all I could about his word. I spent hours reading and studying the bible, then listening to countless teaching tapes at that time. I found books on every subject I was interested in and prayed a lot. If something did not seem right to me, I studied more to see what the word had to say about it. You cannot take everything everyone says at face value because we are all human and capable of making mistakes, that is why it is so important for you to do your own studying of the word. I have always made it a rule that everything I read about God and everything I hear must line up with the word of God, if it doesn't, I put it on the shelve and leave it alone unless the Lord reveals otherwise.

I found that in studying and learning the word I was able to minister to others with accuracy. I never want to deceive anyone knowingly in any way. I have learned to follow my spirit, what drives me, what propels me, and I have found it is teaching people what the Lord reveals to me out of his word.

I used to think God could not use me due to all my failures. I was so timid; I could not see myself speaking in front of people. I used to think that if I were in that kind of position; I would be an open book and people would judge me. I have had to learn not to be afraid of people or what they think. I was so concerned about what people would think that I became an introvert. After going to bible school, the shyness turned into a desire to see lives changed and transformed by the power of God's word and I began to come out of my shell and let down the guard that I had kept up for so long. I became obsessed in helping people see themselves as God sees them, without realizing it my own perception of people was changing and that spirit of timidity disappeared. Oh, it tries to take hold of me again, but I have learned to conquer it. No matter how long one has walked with the Lord, one will continue to be reminded of one's failures, whether by memories, other people, or the enemy who will not let you forget. God will never remind you of your failures. God does not live in the past; God is always now.

God is Awesome

God is awesome and because he is awesome, he does awesome things for those who put their trust in him.

I have witnessed God's miraculous work firsthand, just seeing what he has done in my life is a miracle. God took me from the miry clay and set my feet on solid ground. I had been living such a low life not knowing what God's plan for my life was. Now my foundation is sure, and my feet are planted on the rock. I would never go back to the life I used to live because God has been faithful to his word and he has never let me down, neither is there any desire in me to return to those beggarly elements of the world.

I have seen what faith in God's word can do. I have seen God perform miracles. One example of a miracle is that of my grandson who was run over by a car and left on the sidewalk to die, he sustained a traumatic brain injury and had to have brain surgery. He was kept in a medically induced coma for several weeks to prevent him from moving. I know how the power of agreement and our speaking the same thing works because I have seen it work time and again. We got the family in agreement not to speak anything negative only what we wanted the outcome to be. He had to undergo several serious brain and skull surgeries. The brain surgeons said there were no guarantees of what the outcome would be, he could have brain damage or worse he could die in surgery, but we had inside information. We knew if we stood on the word of God and kept guard over our words, everything was going to be alright. Since the last surgery he had, he is doing very well. He functions just as normal as he did before with no brain damage and no seizures and God gets all the glory.

The Word Works

The bible says God has given us all things which pertain to life and godliness. (*2 Peter 1:3 KJV*) Everything you will ever need is provided in God's word. We must learn how to put God's word to work for us. God creates with his word. In the beginning nothing was created until God spoke the word and it was so. (*Genesis 1:3 KJV*) God is still creating today but he works according to his word spoken out of our mouth. He looks after his word to perform it. The bible says the angels hearken to the voice of his word. (*Psalm 103:20 KJV*) The Spanish bible says they hearken to the word to execute it. Are your angels working for you or are they waiting on you to speak the word? Are your angels unemployed? The bible says they are all ministering spirits sent to minister for those who are heirs of salvation. (*Hebrews 1:14 KJV*) You are an heir of salvation and angels are standing by to execute the word of God when you speak it.

If you want to know God's plan for you begin to quote scriptures that say things like, I am filled with the knowledge of God's will in all wisdom and spiritual understanding, I know what the will of the Lord is. My steps are ordered of the Lord. When you do that those scriptures become real to you and in time you will understand God's will for your life.

We all need wisdom and the bible tells us that wisdom is the principal thing. (*Proverbs 4:7 KJV*) It is the most important thing that we must have, it is wisdom that comes from God that gives us understanding and shows us the best way to handle all situations that arise.

CHAPTER 9

I Am who God's word Says I am

How do You see Yourself?

WE HAVE DISCUSSED seeing ourselves as God sees us and learning to have a right estimation of ourselves. I want to go a little further with that subject because in ministering to women who have been abused, I see a pattern of how abused women see themselves. I know women who are hard on themselves because of feelings and emotions they are experiencing. They hate themselves for the anger that is within. I have found even from my own experience that anger comes from concentrating on the abuse that took place and the longer we are silent about it the more it festers. Many women seem to fall into a pattern of abusive relationships and do not know what to do or how to get out of them. I do not have all the answers, but I know someone who does and that is God.

I used to have so much anger bottled up inside of me for such a long time and I did not understand why I could not be a better person. I can honestly say that when I wrote my first book of Stolen Identity it began a restoration process in me. The Lord brought things to the surface that were kept hidden. I did not want to write a book, I never thought I would. It was the Lord's idea for me to write **Stolen Identity** and he showed me how subtle the enemy is and how he steals people's identities since Adam and Eve's disobedience. Even though I was born again for years, I did not know who I was in Christ.

Has your Identity Been Stolen?

Maybe your identity has been stolen and that is why you see yourself as a failure and unworthy of God's love. You must no longer see yourself that way because your identity has been changed. You have a new identity in Christ, you no longer identify with the past because you are now a new creature. When God looks at you; he only sees who you are in Christ and that is the way he wants you to see yourself.

I did not understand the emotions I had, the anger, the fear, the intimidation and the low estimation I had of myself. I just knew I did not seem to measure up to anyone. There was always something lacking in me. I cried out to God as I am sure you have also, but I still felt trapped in myself. God used the writing of **Stolen Identity** to set me free. It was not easy writing the book, I never wanted anyone to know what had happened to me and how it affected my life, but God had something else in mind, while I was writing the book he was working on me. I believe a person who has been abused in any way thinks people are going to think less of them because of it, so they suffer in silence. It took approximately three years to finish the book, I had to depend on God to lead me as to what to write. It is much easier writing this book because I have been able to minister to abused women and I know that Stolen Identity has helped many and I believe this will do the same.

God is not seeing your failures or your faults. God looks on the heart. (*1 Samuel 16:7 KJV*) We look on the outside appearance and we see all our faults and failures. God created you in his image. It is the enemy who has marred your image of yourself by keeping you concentrating on the things you see as failures remembering the mistakes you have made.

We do not have to go through life wearing a mask in order to make people accept us or see us the way we want them to see us. I did not know how to be myself. I wanted so much to just be me because it is where I felt most comfortable, but I always felt like I had to live up to people's expectations even if it meant being miserable. I did not reach out to anyone for help because I did not know of anyone that I could put my trust in. Today I know that it is not people's opinion of me that matters, but God's

Church is supposed to be the place where you can find help. The church I was attending in the early days of my walk with the Lord, preached condemnation and told us not to do certain things but never told us how to overcome or how to apply the word to our lives. When the Lord called me to teach I was determined that I was going to teach people how to do what the bible says and never to preach condemnation because the bible says *God did not send his Son into the world to condemn the world, but that the world through him might be saved. (John 3:17 KJV)*

Do not ever feel condemned because of what you have been through. God takes those very things the enemy meant to destroy you and uses them so that you can help others who are going through similar situations. Some women I have talked to feel ugly because of the anger inside. They are pent up emotions that have not had a way of release, once released a burden is lifted and you begin to feel free.

Knowing who you are in Christ frees you from condemnation. God made you just the way he wants you, unique in all your ways because he does not want copies. Quit condemning yourself every time you do something wrong, there is no one perfect. You can be confident in who you are, knowing God has great plans for you and the more you grow in him the more you understand your purpose in life.

The only way I can assure you that you will be established in who you are in Christ is by finding scripture that says in him or in whom, they are talking about you. I love to read *Ephesians and Colossians* because I see what Christ has accomplished and how it benefits me. Every time I see "in Christ" I say that is who God says I am.

In order to understand all that Christ has done for us, we must read, meditate and apply the word so that we become established and in so doing we are building a firm foundation that cannot be shaken. God never promised that we would go through life without struggles or trials. He did promise to be with us always and to show us how to overcome and come out victorious over every situation.

God will Establish You

I love what (1 Peter 5:19 Amplified Bible) says. *After you have suffered for a little while, the God of all grace [who imparts His blessing and favor], who called you to His own eternal glory in Christ, will Himself complete, confirm, strengthen, and establish you [making you what you ought to be].*

The bible says after you have suffered for a little while, to us a little while seems like an eternity, he will complete you, confirm you, strengthen you and establish you. Isn't that wonderful? There is hope for us. Suffering happens to us because we live in a fallen world and we have an enemy and life is not easy, but through the word of God we conquer every enemy that revolts against us

What does it mean to be complete? The Webster dictionary says, complete means having all the necessary or appropriate parts. It means to make you whole. Then he will confirm you. To confirm you means that you will be established in the truth or correctness of something previously believed, suspected, or feared to be the case.

All I can say is, what a relief it is to know the truth and to be set free from the lies of the enemy and the lies I believed about myself. The bible says he will strengthen you and make you more effective in life. Last of all he will establish you in the faith, in the word, in the acceptance of who you are in him, in believing in yourself and accepting who God says you are as an established fact.

I marvel at the goodness of God and my Lord Jesus Christ. I have come to know him as my firm foundation. He is the rock on which I stand. His word is what has given me a firm foundation so that I am no longer moved by what people say or think because I know in whom I have believed, and I know what the word says about me. I have spent enough time in the word so that I have come to know how good and wonderful God is.

Some people ask, how can you say you know God? My answer is I know him through my Lord and Savior Jesus Christ. *The bible says Jesus is the image of the invisible God. (Colossians 1:15 NKJV.) (Hebrews 1:3 KJV)* says *He is the express image of His person,* Jesus said *"if you have seen me, you have seen the Father.* (John 14:9 *KJV)* You must come to know God through a personal relationship with him, through your relationship with Jesus Christ. Jesus is a God of compassion, a God of love, a God of forgiveness, a faithful God, one who cannot lie. You can only come to know him by spending time with him, in the word and spending time getting to know him through the time you spend with him in prayer. He wants to be your personal savior, the one who died for you so that you can have new life and have it more abundantly.

God chooses the foolish things of this world

> *But God hath chosen the foolish things of this world to confound the wise; and God hath chosen the weak things of this world to confound the things which are mighty; the base things of the world, and things which are despised, hath God chosen, yea, and things which are not, to bring to naught things that are: That no flesh should glory in his presences. (1 Corinthians 1:27 KJV)*

God uses the base things of the world and things that are despised. Many times, a person feels like they have nothing to offer, that their life is not worth much because they see themselves through eyes of failure. Those are the very ones God choses to confound the wise, the educated, the smart ones by world standards. It takes a humble person for God to work with because he can mold and make that one into what he or she was meant to be. When the world sees failure, God sees potential. God did not create any human being without potential. Sometimes all it takes to bring out that potential is someone caring, someone saying, you are important, believe in yourself, you can do it.

Maybe you were raised in a home where there was no encouragement to give you hope or a desire to become something in life and you spent your life looking for that encouragement from somebody, anybody who would just say kind words to you. That is why I believe it is so important to speak words of encouragement to our children so that they do not have to look for encouragement in all the wrong places. Many people end up in what some call the junk heap or in ashes, because they never received the encouragement they needed as a child.

I didn't grow up in a Christian home, my family didn't deny God, but they didn't know any better, all they did was pass on the religion they were brought up in, so I didn't receive any encouragement from my parents as a result I was a shy intimidated child. I remember growing up believing in God and praying the only way I knew how. My younger brother and I spent a lot of time playing outside. My parents did not say much to us. My dad was a man of few words. When I came to the Lord; I found the fulfillment I had been seeking. It was not my parent's fault; they like many parents did not know any better, but they did their best with what they knew.

Rosie Rivera

My fulfillment comes from my relationship with the Lord and from ministering his word and helping others find God's will for their life through study and a personal relationship with the Lord. There will never be anything more fulfilling than the time you spend getting to know the Lord and all that he has done for you. In God's word you will find your identity, you will find acceptance and a love that never fails.

CHAPTER 10

Be Patient, God is not Finished with You

But let patience have its perfect work, that you may be perfect and complete, lacking nothing. (James 1:4 KJV)

WHAT A WONDERFUL statement! When the word let is used in a sentence, you are the understood subject. You have something to do with patience having its perfect work. We all want to be perfect and entire, lacking nothing, but getting to that place takes patience and that in turn takes time and work. The bible tells us that *the trying of our faith is what works patience.* (James 1:3 *KJV*)

Some say they do not like to ask God for patience because it seems like every time, they ask for patience they end up with things coming against them. We would have to live in a perfect world to never have tests and trials in life. Those things that come against us are the very things that we must learn to get the victory over, as we do, patience is being developed and we are on our way to maturity and completeness.

Patience is something you grow into as you grow in Christ. It is something that must be practiced with those who are difficult to get along with. We can see by observing a child how impatience displays itself since birth. Patience comes as they begin to understand they cannot have everything they want when they want it. For a Christian it comes as we grow in knowledge and understanding of God's word.

Growing up as a Christian is a process. We are not born again one day and a complete mature Christian the next. The bible says as new born babes we are *to desire the sincere milk of the word that we may grow thereby.(1 Peter 2:2 KJV)* Just as a new born goes from being totally taken care of, having everything done for them and then progresses to a toddler, then a child, then a teen and finally an adult so it is with a new born again Christian.

There are people who get born again, on fire for God, be overly anxious to do something for God but one must be patient, everything works out in its time. When I got born again; I was one of those who wanted to do something but did not know what to do. I could not help anyone because I had no knowledge of the word all I knew was that I was in love with the Lord. Even with the little Robert and I knew we were able to help several people come to accept Jesus despite our ignorance, but we could not take them any further because we did not have enough knowledge or understanding of the word.

Have you noticed how that it is the newborn Christians who want to get everyone else saved? They are so excited about their newly found love that they want everyone to experience the same. It is so sad that many Christians sit in church for years without ever telling anyone about the Lord or ever inviting anyone to church, but the new Christians want everyone to go to church and meet Jesus. When we got saved, we talked to everyone we could think of in our small community inviting them to church. On April Fool's day of 1979, we had 40 people baptized in the little Baptist church we got born again in. The church had never seen so many baptized in one day. Many of those who were born again, went on to become pastors and establish churches.

Once you receive Jesus as your Lord and Savior the next step is to begin reading the bible so that you can grow in the knowledge of God. I suggest you begin reading the New Testament before you try to understand the Old Testament. The Old Testament is the New Testament concealed and the New Testament is the Old Testament revealed. I recommend reading (*Ephesians 1:15 to 23 KJV)* It is a prayer the Apostle Paul prayed for the Ephesians after he became aware of their faith in the Lord. It is a prayer you can pray for yourself. I have made it a practice to pray this prayer for myself. I need wisdom and revelation in the knowledge of God. I need the eyes of my understanding enlightened and I must know the hope of my calling before I can begin to fulfill God's plan for my life.

Some think it is hard being a Christian, but the bible says it is the way of the transgressor that is hard. Sometimes it just takes hindsight to see where we came from and recognize how good we have it now. I would not trade this life for anything. I know from experience that the way of the transgressor is hard. (*Proverbs 13:15 KJV*) I have been there, done that, but thank God for his mercy and grace that translated me out of that kingdom of darkness and now I see and live in the light.

What is Patience?

One of the definitions of patience is to endure discomfort without complaint. For this it requires other virtues such as self-control, humility and generosity. The cliché that patience is a virtue is true to a certain extent, but patience does not stand alone without the other virtues that make up patience. (*Galatians 5:22,23 KJV*) lists patience as one of the fruits of the spirit, so patience is one of the virtues we acquire as we learn to walk with the Lord.

Refusing to complain in difficult situations requires self-control which is also a fruit of the spirit. It seems like a hard thing to do practicing patience or exercising self-control. Since they are fruits of the spirit; they are not traits of the human nature. When we got born again; we received a new spirit, but we still must deal with our humanity by changing the way we think and learning to think the way God thinks. When Adam and Eve disobeyed God in the Garden of Eden their spirit became separated from the life of God and man began to reason and it is our human reasoning many times that gets us into trouble.

Patience always requires waiting, for example, waiting in line at the supermarket requires patience, waiting in traffic, waiting for someone to get ready, instead of becoming inpatient we practice waiting without complaining. Waiting is difficult because we all struggle with different temptations and we all have different strengths and weaknesses. We become annoyed with the actions of others at times because of our lack of patience.

Waiting on God

For me personally the hardest kind of waiting is waiting on God. God's timing is not my timing. God is not in as much of a hurry as I am. He can see the end from the beginning while we only see the beginning. That is why we end up frustrated, discouraged and become inpatient and end up stepping out ahead of God and doing things on our own that we later regret. It would be wonderful if we could know what the end-result would be before we begin our waiting. Waiting on God requires faith and to exercise faith in waiting one must surrender the final control one has to God which is not an easy thing to do. We are accustomed to being in control of our own life and to surrender every aspect of it is not an easy thing to do.

We must be patient and remember that God is working in us, also in others, none of us have arrived. We must learn not to irritate others with some of the things we do and say or the way that we respond. It takes time to develop patience

As we wait in faith to see the manifestation of what we are waiting for it produces strength and ability to stand knowing that God looks after his word to perform it.

Jesus is our example. He demonstrated patience with his disciples. They sometimes were hard-headed and argued about who would be the greatest. They did not understand why he had to die. Peter rebuked him when he tried to tell them about what was about to happen to him. When Jesus was asleep in the boat and a storm arose, they assumed that he did not care that they were drowning. Jesus had to exercise patience with them knowing they were only human with human frailties.

Just think of the patience Jesus exercised in knowing that Judas was going to betray him and yet gave him a place in his ministry as he did the others. The bible says Jesus knew from the beginning who was going to betray him. (*John 13:11 KJV*) It could not have been easy on him knowing that the one who was going to betray him was one of the chosen, yet he treated him no different than the others.

Jesus lived in a state of patience knowing the purpose for which he had come and waiting for that day to approach. We can see his agony in the garden as he prayed for a possible way of escaping what lay ahead with no response from his Father even though he prayed earnestly that if it was at all possible, God would take that cup from him. After intense prayer he said, *"not my will but yours be done,"* (*Luke 22:42 KJV*) surrendering his will to the Father so that when the soldiers were beating him, he never opened his mouth. He endured the pain of the cross for you. He looked ahead in time and he saw you. He saw your pain and he saw your need; he saw what the end of his suffering would produce, and it helped him endure the cross. What a wonderful Savior we serve!!

The bible says God waits patiently for the fruit of the earth. He does not desire that any man perish so he waits patiently for men to repent and turn from their wicked ways.

> *The Lord is not slack concerning his promise, as some men count slackness; but is longsuffering to us-ward, not willing that any should perish, but that all should come to repentance. (2 Peter 3:9 KJV)*

Patience is a virtue when exercised for a right cause. Our Lord had a cause. He came with a purpose to save us from our sinful nature which we acquired from Adam and Eve's disobedience. Have you stopped to think at any time just how long God waited for the perfect timing to send Jesus? The plan was already in motion since the foundation of the world. Even before man sinned God had already prepared provision to save mankind. The bible says God is long-suffering.

Patience is the ability to keep your cool when you feel like tearing someone apart. People are not always easy to get along with. There will always be people who rub us the wrong way. We always have opportunities to practice being patient with those who are hard to get along with. There is no short cut to developing patience, it is something that must be exercised daily. While we are around human beings, our patience will be tried.

> *Through faith and patience, we inherit the promises. (Hebrews 6:12 KJV)*

To develop patience, we must learn endurance. God never promised us a life without problems. Problems are a part of life that is why developing patience is necessary. The bible says *many are the afflictions of the righteous. but the Lord delivers them out of them all. (Psalm 34:19 KJV)*

> *Jesus said, in the world you will have tribulation but be of good cheer, I have overcome the world. (John 16:33 NKJV)*

The more we develop patience the less the devil has he can work with. The Apostle Paul endured many tests and trials and through it all, he came to understand the grace of God and to trust him to deliver him out of every situation he encountered. God's grace is always available to us, when we are weak, he is strong. No matter what the devil throws at you, you can endure because God's grace is enough for you. No matter how impossible the situation may seem, you must always remember God specializes in impossibilities. They are not impossible to God, but they are so overwhelming to us so that we see them as impossibilities.

Patience and endurance are God qualities. Everything worth having is worth fighting for. It is through patience and endurance that you become steadfast and unmovable in your faith.

It is possible for you to endure anything and everything that comes your way because the greater one lives in you.

(1 Corinthians 13 KJV) is called the love chapter. It is called the love chapter because it shows us what the God kind of love is. One of the characteristics of that love is patience. God is love, he doesn't have love, his love has been shed abroad in our hearts by the Holy Spirit so that we have no excuse for not practicing love and being able to walk in his kind of love.

Jesus gave us one commandment, that we should love one another as he has loved us.

> *A new commandment I give unto you, that ye love one another; as I have loved you. (John 13:34 KJV)*

We have seen what his love is like through the things he endured and the patience he exercised while he walked on the earth. His example is the one we must follow.

You are probably thinking, what does that have to do with my situation? Everything, it is through his love for you that you can overcome the pain of the past. It is through your exercising faith in all that Jesus done for you, that you are now capable of forgiving those who have wronged you. It is not all about us, we think it is all about us, but Jesus showed us a better way and that is the way of love. He taught us to walk in love and forgiveness and how to let go of our selfishness and think of others so we can help them through our experiences and our ability to overcome through Christ. We cannot spend the rest of our lives feeling sorry for ourselves because of things that took place in the past.

Our world is full of hurting people who have gone through terrible things and yet survived. Today we see a world in turmoil. People are beginning to revolt against injustice, some are being killed in their effort to see justice done while others are destroying the foundations of our nation. It seems that people everywhere are protesting for a good cause or a bad one or just protesting to get in on what is happening in the world.

In visiting a poor country one can see the poverty and filth some people must live in. It makes one think of how fortunate we are and how blessed we are to live in America. It causes us to forget about ourselves and our pain and have compassion on the less fortunate.

I would not be writing this book if the Lord had not ministered to me and taught me how to let go and let God minister to me through his word. It is the truth of God's word that has made me free and it will make you free also. God understands you like nobody else can.

I believe that as you have been reading this book you have begun to change the way you think about the past and have closed that chapter of your life and have begun a brand-new chapter.

Now you are beginning a new day, a new journey that consists of so much more as you grow in patience with yourself and others. You are finding that things that bothered you so much in the past no longer have a pull on you because you have a new mind set.

CHAPTER 11

Running the Race

I have fought a good fight, I have finished my course, I have kept the faith: Henceforth there is laid up for me a crown of righteousness, which the Lord, the righteous judge, shall give me at that day: and not to me only, but unto all them also that love his appearing. (2 Timothy 4:7,8 KJV)

THE APOSTLE PAUL as he was approaching the end of his ministry made this statement, I have fought a good fight, I have finished my course, I have kept the faith. That is something every believer should endeavor to do. This scripture informs us that life is a fight, not against one another but overcoming the obstacles the enemy places in our path. You have a course to run, I have a course to run, we do not all run the same course but when we reach the finish line, we all receive a crown.

The good fight

A good fight is always the one we win. The Apostle Paul fought a good fight because he learned to trust God and his grace and not to depend on his own strength to fight his battles. The Apostle Paul suffered many things at the hands of unbelievers. You can read the accounts of his sufferings in the book of Acts. The Apostle Paul persecuted Christians because he was trained as a Pharisee and as a Pharisee, he knew the law, he did not know the Lord. But we can see in the book of Acts that when he met the Lord on the road to Damascus his life was suddenly changed from a Pharisee to a follower of Jesus. In the same way that he had followed the law wholeheartedly he followed Jesus with his whole heart. Not everyone has the glorious conversion that the Apostle Paul had. The Apostle Paul was a chosen vessel of the Lord, the Lord appeared to him and the Lord spoke to him about the things he would suffer for the cause of Christ. One thing about the Apostle Paul he was determined to follow the Lord wherever it took him. That determination kept him in the fight even when it looked easier to give up and quit.

We on the other hand give up too easily, we stay in the fight while everything is going our way, but it's a different story when things get tough and the enemy is breathing down our neck, threatening our life. What is going to keep you in the fight? What is going to keep you going when everything seems to be coming against you? Are you going to quit or fight the good fight of faith?

A boxer in the ring is sometimes knocked down but he is trained not to stay down but to get up and continue the fight, We are sometimes different in that if we get knocked down in life, we see it as the end instead of getting up, and staying in the fight. We should have the mindset that says, I might get knocked down but never knocked out.

Determination to Run

Determination to run your race as the bible says, with patience, *looking unto Jesus the author and the finisher of your faith* is what will keep you in the race. (*Hebrews12:2 KJV*) the bible also says *consider Jesus.* (*Hebrews 12:3 KJV*) Have you considered him and all that he endured? Have you considered the fact that he knew he would one day suffer for all mankind and still agreed to do it? Have you considered the pain he suffered being an innocent man who had done no wrong yet took upon himself the punishment for sin he never committed? Jesus endured the pain and the cross for you and me. What are you willing to endure for his sake?

We must stop allowing our past mistakes to take our focus away from the Lord. If we are going to run this race to the finish line, we must make Jesus our priority, letting go of those things that so easily beset us and turn our eyes upon Him, Stay focused.

How do we make our fight a good one? In order to ensure that your fight will be a good one you must meditate in the word and let it dwell richly in you, studying to show yourself approved and rightly dividing the word of truth. It is of utmost importance that we know the word of God and that we not only have a mental assent to what it means, but to have revelation of it which then gives us the ability to apply it to our life and our situations. The word of God has all the answers to every question you will ever have, but if the bible is sitting on the coffee table gathering dust, it cannot help you when you are facing a crisis.

The bible tells us that *the weapons of our warfare are not carnal, but they are mighty through God to the pulling down of strongholds. (2 Corinthians 10:4 KJV)* The strongholds that we are to pull down are the strongholds that we have accumulated in our minds though traditions, through lies, through religion, through things that we believed. Maybe one of the things that you have believed is that you have no worth, God can't use you because you have failed him time and again, but when you look into the word you begin to see that those were lies that you believed but now the word of God has set you free and you know that God is a good God, a forgiving God and a faithful God. The word gives you a confidence you did not have before and it causes you to believe you can do all things through Christ who strengthens you.

You are no longer bound by lies the enemy put in your head. You now know the truth and the truth has made you free to be the person God created you to be. There is a race that has been set before you and how you run it is going to determine whether you reach the finish line triumphantly or not.

How you run your race will determine how you finish. If we keep our eyes focused on Jesus, we have the guarantee that we are running well and that we will reach the finish-line without losing our faith.

As I look around me and observe people in many churches, I see the lack of teaching where trusting and believing God is concerned. Some ministers say, have faith in God, all you need is faith, but never tell you how to get it or how to have faith and the people continue to fill prayer lines. I am thankful for Rhema because it taught me faith. The bible says the just shall live by faith. Faith is a lifestyle of trusting the word of God and believing that God is not a man that he should lie but that God's word is truth.

Where do I get Faith?

Faith comes as we hear God's word and as we meditate in it and continue in it. Faith does not come from heaving heard as I have mentioned once before. I also mentioned that the bible says without faith it is impossible to please God. I believe every Christian wants to please God and to trust him and his word but many times the tests and trials of life choke the word and it is not capable of producing the desired results. The bible teaches us to protect our heart, to guard it above all because out of it flow the issues of life, or the sources of life.

It is so easy to get sidetracked from the important things in life and to get caught up in what is going on around us. You can tell where someone is by listening to him talk because out of the abundance of the heart the mouth speaks according to the bible.

Many Christians are still carnal or immature in their Christian walk. Their speech is as the speech of those who do not know the Lord. Their speech is always negative. When one's mind is renewed by the word, one trains one's self to say what the word says and not what is seen, felt or heard. As we speak God's word, faith is rising in our heart.

Finishing Your Course

Are you satisfied with where you are in life at this point in your walk with God? Is there still room for improvement? There will always be room for improvement while we are alive. Being content with where we are will keep us from pressing on to better things. God will allow you to stay where you're at, but if you want to go further with him you will have to fight the good fight of faith. Do you want to go further than you have ever been before? God is wanting to take you to higher levels with him. You must be ready to fight for what you want because every time God takes you higher the devil comes to interfere with what God is doing in your life.

God has a plan for your life, you are not an accident. God formed and fashioned you in your mother's womb. You are valuable, you are a joint in the body of Christ and the body increases with the supply of every joint. We all need one another, because each one of us is a joint that supplies nourishment to the rest of the body. There are some things you are not going to get any other way than from that which you can get from other joints in the body of Christ.

The body of Christ was intended to function as one body with many members. We do not all have the same calling or the same anointing. Yes, we are all anointed by the Holy Spirit, but our functions are different. The bible says *the gifts of the Spirit function as he wills not as we will. (1 Corinthians 12:11 KJV)* We cannot turn them on and off any time we want to. It is written in *(John 14:16* and *John 16:13 KJV)* that he would send us another comforter who would be with us always and would lead us into all truth and would show us things to come. We must learn to be led by the Holy Spirit. He speaks to us through our recreated spirit, sometimes you will feel a nudging or a prompting in your spirit, it is the Holy Spirit wanting to lead you to do something or to cause you to become aware of something you can't see that could mislead you or deceive you. He can warn you of something you cannot see coming so that you can begin to pray and avoid it.

Do you have a vision of God's plan for your life? The word says without a vision the people perish. What do you want out of life? Many people miss out on God's best because they are content to live a mediocre life. They do not press into what God has for them therefore they live in frustration and miss out on what God is doing.

There is more to the Christian life than just going to church. Church is where we learn about God and his word. We do not come to church because it pleases God. It pleases God when we come to church to learn how to become a doer of the word and continue to grow and become a useful part of God's plan. That is where we learn how to overcome in life and how to get along with all people. I am sure you have met and know people who are hard to get along with. When we learn to walk in the God kind of love, we can learn how to love them also.

God's word produces a vision in our heart and vision propels us forward into a deeper walk with God. As we see ourselves as God sees us, we are being changed. God's word helps you to let go of the things that have been hindering you and teaches you to take hold of what God has provided for you. You want to grow so that you do not want to quit and give up every time you meet resistance. Remember we talked about the children of Israel and how they were ok if things were going their way but as soon as they encountered resistance they began to murmur and complain because of the way. It is when we encounter resistance that we must press toward the mark. It is when we are met with resistance that we gain persistence.

We live in a real world where we are going to come across many things that we do not necessarily like but we are not

Rosie Rivera

going to allow the things we don't like to keep us from running our race well.

The apostle Paul said we should run to obtain the price not as one who beats the air. Beating the air gets us nowhere, but if we keep our eyes focused on the price we will run with patience and one day that patience will pay off.

It is better to try something than to try nothing and succeed. We cannot let the fear of failure keep us from reaching our goal. We can let failures become a weight or we can use them as wings to mount up on and accomplish goals we did not think we could. Many of the successes we see in the world today came after several attempts that failed because they kept pressing forward.

CHAPTER 12

Guarding Your Heart

Keep your heart with all diligence for out of it
spring the issues of life. (Proverbs 4:23 NKJV)

What Does Keep Your Heart, Mean?

*I*T MEANS THAT you guard your heart against things that keep you from receiving God's best. If you don't guard your heart, the enemy will begin bringing old thoughts to your mind and if you dwell on them long enough they will begin to contaminate your heart and before you know it you will become depressed and discouraged and begin to think God doesn't love you and you will go right back to the place where you were before Jesus set you free, right back into bondage.

What do we guard our hearts against? One thing that we must guard our heart against is offense. Jesus said offenses will come, but woe to him through whom they come. (*Luke 17:1 KJV*) Offense breeds every kind of evil. It breeds resentment, anger, bitterness, strife and un-forgiveness. If we can recognize an offense when it comes, we can guard our heart from the bad fruit it produces.

Have you ever been offended? I am sure you have; we all have experienced offense. How did it affect you? How do you feel when you run into the person who offended you? Do you bless them and pray for them or do all those feelings and thoughts produced by the offence rush back into you mind? Maybe you see them from a distance in the grocery store and go to another part of the store to avoid having an encounter with them. When you have really forgiven, the sting is no longer there.

We all have opportunities to become offended because we are human, and we have feelings and emotions that make it easy to become offended or take up another's offense. Have you ever had a friend or family member who was offended at someone? What happened when that person related the reason for the offense to you? We often take up their offense even though that person did us no wrong.

The word of God teaches us to be in control of our feelings and emotions and not to allow them to control us. When guarding our heart, we are learning how to respond to situations that could be offensive.

The bible says we can be angry if we do not sin in our anger. (*Ephesians 4:26 KJV*) We can be angry at injustice and unrighteousness, we can feel anger when we see the suffering in our world, but we can do something about those things by allowing the word of God to lead us. The bible says, *For the wrath of man does not produce the righteousness of God.* (James 1:20 *NKJV)* The word of God will constrain you.

The devil uses offenses as a bait to entrap you. He will bring a situation or situations into your life with the potential to cause strife and offense, but it is up to you take the bait or leave it.

Where is Your Heart?

We can recognize where one's heart is by what comes out of their mouth. *Out of the abundance of the heart the mouth speaks. (Matthew 12:35 KJV).* What is coming out of your mouth? Have you ever stopped and listened to yourself speak? Are the words you are speaking bringing edification to the hearer?

One does not have to be around a person for long to locate where that person's thinking is. Have you ever been around people where you feel like you need to take a spiritual bath? Everything that comes out of their mouth is filth. You can walk into a room where strife is or has been and you can sense the tension. Those spirits of strife and offense will try to attach themselves to you and soon you will find yourself in strife with someone taking up another's offense that had nothing to do with you. Jesus told his disciples, be careful how you hear. Many times, we do not clearly hear the way we should because our heart is hardened, or we have a wounded heart and we hear things in a wrong way and not like they were intended.

The Ear, a Gateway to The Heart

The ear is one of the gateways to the heart. It is easy to pick up someone's offense just by hearing without knowing what the whole situation is all about, especially if it is coming from someone close to you. We have all been in situations where someone says something, and we take it wrong. When that happens, how does it make you feel? Sometimes we take it as a put down or as a reminder of our failures. The bible instructs us to guard what we hear or how we hear.

God delivers us from all the ugly things of our past and then he expects us to fill ourselves with the word so that we are in control of every situation. Have you noticed when a parking lot has been vacant for some length of time it begins to revert to its original state? Weeds begin to pop up out of the cracks in the concrete. The word of God instructs us to guard our heart with all diligence because if we do not guard it, the things we have been redeemed from begin to creep back in. It does not happen suddenly. It is a subtle process and before you know it you find yourself saying and doing things you thought were a thing of the past.

Attend unto my words, incline your ear unto my sayings. (Proverbs 4:20 KJV) Jesus always said to his disciples, take heed to my sayings which is to pay attention to, to meditate, to ponder. It is important that we pay attention to what we hear and how we hear. We must filter what we hear because faith for positive things comes by hearing so does faith for negative things come by hearing.

> *For the word of God is quick, and powerful, and sharper than any two-edged sword, piercing even to the dividing asunder of soul and spirit, and of the joints and marrow, and is a discerner of the thoughts and intents of the heart. (Hebrews 4:12 KJV)*

You are probably thinking, what does this have to do with the things I am going through? It has a much to do with what you are going through, because your heart has been contaminated with negative thoughts about yourself. Now that God has set you free there are negative feelings and emotions that you must guard your heart against so that the enemy cannot bring you down with thoughts of failure and defeat. You do not want those thoughts to become something you continue to meditate on until they become strongholds in your mind. Once a thought becomes an imagination and you continue to dwell on it, it is on its way to becoming a stronghold.

I mentioned earlier that the mind is the battleground where we either win or lose our battles. A thought can become a stronghold, the more you think on it, the more control it has on how you react and before you know it, it begins to produce negative fruit in your life. God sets us free, but it is up to us to work at staying free.

The apostle Paul said he exercised himself to keep a conscience void of offense toward God and man. You can be offended at God because maybe he did not come through for you when you wanted him to, or his answer was not what you wanted to hear. God knows what we need, and he is ever ready to meet all our needs but not all our wants. What may not seem like an answer to you at the time, may be exactly what you need.

The Eyes, a Gateway to the Heart

The eyes are another gateway to the heart. We must be careful what we allow our eyes to see. If we see something long enough, it begins to form an image on the inside of our heart. The bible instructs us to look right on, do not turn to the right or to the left but stay focused. What you allow your eyes to see affects you either positively or negatively.

In this age of technology and the internet, we must guard our eyes in what we allow ourselves to see. People do not become hooked on pornography because it comes across their screen once. They get hooked when they continually allow their eyes to see it because it makes them feel good and gives the flesh a certain satisfaction. The devil knows exactly how to bring one into bondage. Wisdom says, stay away from things that contaminate your heart, be careful what you allow yourself to see. The internet is not bad, it is what we allow into our homes through what we watch that brings about confusion and loose morals. If we do not see anything wrong with sex on TV or drugs and are not selective about what we allow our children to watch, they grow up thinking there is nothing wrong with it. Eventually what one sees will get into one's heart. We must guard the gateways to our heart.

There are so many things our eyes can see today that were not allowed before, so much information coming into our homes that it is easy to allow those things to take our eyes off of the important things in life. We can become calloused in our thinking. We do not want our heart to become hardened by what we allow our eyes to see.

What we Say

The tongue causes us more trouble than any other member of our body. What we say can either produce success, or defeat. Whatever is in our heart in abundance is going to come out of our mouth.

Life and death are in the power of the tongue. (Proverbs 18:21 KJV) The tongue is such a small member of the body, yet it can cause great damage. We can use it to speak life or we can use it to speak death. That is why we must guard what comes out of our mouth.

Words Carry Power

Even so the tongue is a little member, and boasteth great things. Behold, how great a matter a little fire kindleth! And the tongue is a fire, a world of

> *iniquity: so is the tongue among our members,*
> *that it defileth the whole body, and setteth on fire*
> *the course of nature; and it is set on fire of hell.*
> *(James 3:5,6 KJV)*

To get the full impact about the power of the tongue you must read James chapter 3. It speaks about how powerful the tongue is. James says if we offend not in word, we are a mature person, we choose what we say before we speak. The course of your life is set by the words you speak,

Many people fail in life because of words that impacted them in their childhood. You will never amount to anything, you are no good for nothing, you cannot do anything right. Those words go down in their heart and control their actions. It dictates how they act and respond. It sets them up for failure. That is why it is so important that we speak words of life, words that encourage and build up rather than words that tear down and wound their spirits.

Maybe you were brought up that way and that is why you have such a low self-image. You do not have to continue believing a lie. God created you for great things. Let him change the course of your life. We have all heard the saying, sticks and stones may break my bones, but words will never hurt me. According to the bible that is not true. Words go down into the innermost part of our being and can become wounds in our spirit.

The spirit of man will sustain his infirmity; but a wounded spirit who can bear (Proverbs 18:14 KJV)

Words are containers of spiritual power and they can work in the negative or in the positive. Words have creative power. That is why the bible has so much to say concerning words.

When a lawyer is defending a person, he always advices the client not to say anything that will incriminate him because it can be used against him in a court of law. What you say can be used against you by the enemy, your words can make you or break you. The devil will take your negative words and use them to destroy you.

We can speak faith which God responds to or we can speak fear which the devil responds to. Guard your heart by what you say. You can give God something to work with or you can give the devil something to work with. God works with positive words; the devil works with negative words. Positive words work for you, negative words work against you. God framed the worlds with his word, we can also frame our world with our words.

Guard Your Heart from Unforgiveness

Unforgiveness is an enemy to your heart and to your soul. Unforgiveness keeps a person in bondage to the past. The hardest person to forgive is one's self. One's heart knows its own bitterness. Things that were done to one in the past can become embedded wounds that can fester and bleed until one pours the healing word of God into the wound and we realize that we must forgive, not for the benefit of the person who wronged us but for our own healing.

Healing will not begin until you forgive. When you do not forgive, you keep the wound open and every time you are reminded of the past that wound begins to bleed again. But when you seal that wound through forgiveness it begins to close the wound and when thoughts come, they can't affect you anymore because you have let go of that which is causing the infection. Hurting people hurt other people and many times it is those who are closest to us that we hurt.

> *Jesus said when you stand praying forgive so that your heavenly Father can also forgive you your trespasses. (Mark 11:25 KJV)*

I struggled with many different emotions because I did not know there was a root cause to my problems. I kept putting a band aide over the wound, but it would never stick long enough for the wound to heal until I learned to forgive myself for what I blamed myself for even though I was the one who was wronged. Thank God for his love and his mercy. Thank God for the word that set me free and put me on the right track. Thank God that I learned that forgiveness benefits me when I choose to forgive.

I believe that when you choose to forgive whoever wronged you and then forgive yourself God will come and heal your wounds so that you can begin the rest of your life with the assurance that God loves you, has forgiven you, has accepted you and you are no longer the person you used to be.

You will find that the past no longer has control over you because you no longer identify yourself with the past, now you identify yourself with who God created you to be. You have a new image and a new life, and you will never doubt God's love for you. Now when you look in the mirror you no longer see that shy intimidated person, you now see a confident person, a bold person, a person who can stand tall, one who believes that you were created for such a time as this, blessed and highly favored of God, created in His image.

CHAPTER 13

Love, God's Way

Jesus said to him, "you shall love the Lord your God with all your heart, with all your soul, and with all your mind. This is the first and great commandment. And the second is like it: You shall love your neighbor as yourself. On these two commandments hang all the law and the Prophets." (Matthew 22:37 to 40 KJV)

First things first

G OD LOVED US before we ever loved him. He sent his only begotten son into the world to save his creation. Sin separated us from God when Adam and Eve sinned in the garden of Eden. God in his love made a way for us to get back into a relationship with God. Before man sinned, God came down in the cool of the day to walk with Adam and Eve and fellowship with them but when they disobeyed God and ate of the forbidden fruit, it caused a separation between them so he had to drive them out of the garden so that they would not eat from the tree of life and live forever in a fallen state. God made provision long before man sinned. The scripture says, we should love the Lord our God with all our heart, soul and mind, that means with everything that is in us. He gave his all for us therefore we must give our all for him, not holding anything back. It is easy to love God because he is perfect, there are no flaws in him, and his love is pure. It is his creation that we have problems with.

We must learn to love God's way. It is easy for us to love somebody when they are sweet and nice, and everything is going our way, but God's way is so much better. It is harder to love God's way because it requires not only effort but discipline on our part. God's way requires us to love those who are not kind to us, those who do not agree with us, those who despitefully use us, those who say bad things about us.

God is love. He does not have love, love is the very essences of God, it is what God is. We are born with a need to be loved and many times when what we thought was love goes wrong, we get the wrong idea about what love is all about. Just because somebody failed you or mistreated you does not mean you cannot know real love. The bible describes what the God kind of love is. It is so different from what we think love is supposed to be

(I Corinthians 13:4-7 NKJV)

Love suffers long and is kind; love does not envy; love does not parade itself, is not puffed up; does not behave rudely, does not seek its own, is not

provoked, thinks no evil; does not rejoice in iniquity, but rejoices in truth; bears all things, believes all things, hopes all things, endures all things. First part of verse 8 says: Love never fails.

To love God's way seems like a hard thing to do because human love is so unreliable, human love goes by how one feels, it goes by looks, by emotions which can sometimes be misleading. The God kind of love will never mislead you but will guide you into doing the right thing. Sometimes we just need to stop a minute and ask our self, am I responding in love or am I acting out of selfishness? Human love is selfish, it does not think of the other person first. Human love is motivated by the five physical senses.

I used to think love for me was something I could never attain. I did not have parents who expressed love to us children. My mother who passed in 1991, was given to an aunt when she was just a baby and she always felt unloved because she couldn't understand why her mother gave her away and kept the six other children she had, so she always had that question in her mind. I believe that is what kept her from being able to express love. It was later in life, after coming to the Lord that my mother began to express love to us. My father did not show much affection either. I guess I grew up not knowing what it felt like to be loved. Thank God for his word, because through it I came to understand what real love is.

If one does not study the word of God, then one cannot know the depth of God's love and what Jesus went through to set humanity free. I believe the reason many people never grow up spiritually is because they do not study on their own, therefore they do not have a revelation of the word of God to be able to understand the love of God.

A teacher of the word is God ordained to equip the people for the work of the ministry so that they are not led astray by false teachers or doctrines of man rather the word of God. Maybe it is because I am a teacher that I feel so strongly about teaching. It grieves me when I see people being led astray and going through things they should not have to go through. The bible says, my people perish for a lack of knowledge. I can see that now. because I am now able to see how it has been through knowledge that I do not have to accept living a life of defeat.

There are those who seem to always be seeking for something and never finding what they are looking for, they go from one church to another but never seem to settle down in one place. Those people are unstable because they are not being taught the word of God and they are not spending time in the word on their own. The word of God establishes the Christian, so he is not led astray because of the strong foundation one has that keeps him on track. It is of utmost importance that one has a firm foundation of the word of God because when everything is being shaken one can stand firm and unmovable trusting in the Lord.

God's word has all the answers to everything you are going through. It gets you through the tough times, it shows you how to be victorious and how to overcome in life. It teaches you how to get victory over your circumstances.

I truly believe that if it had not been for the word of God in my life, I would have given up, I would have quit many times but his word has kept me anchored and steady in the storms of life. Tough times are not over just because we are Christians and study the word, we must put it into practice in our life by not only being a hearer but being a doer of it. It has not always been easy. There have been times even in ministry when I have wanted to tuck tail and run, to move away, to quit but the love of God always compelled me to continue. There have been times when I would have liked to walk away from the problems of life, but it is not always that easy. It is easier to stay in the fight and fight the good fight of faith. It is always a good fight because we win.

Even in Christian circles, it is sometimes hard to love everybody because not everyone is lovely. We all have faults. Love must be a choice. It must be a choice that we make, a determination to love God's people because he first loved us and his love for us is an unconditional love. The bible says we must love one another, it does not give us a choice. God loved us while we were sinners how much more, does he love us now that we have been reconciled to him.

God's love has never failed me, each time I call upon him, he hears and answers me.

I don't always get the answer I want to hear but I always get what I need.

The scripture on love, says that love never fails, since God is love, he can never fail.

When we walk in love with one another, we are practicing what the word says and it pleases God when we obey. The bible says we have passed from death to life because we love the brethren. *(1 John 3:14 NKJV)*

Jesus told us to have love one to another. He is not asking us to love in our own strength or ability, he graces us to do it because his love has been shed abroad in our heart by the Holy Spirit so that we are able to depend on his love and not our own. God's grace is what enables you and me to do the things we cannot do in our own strength or ability.

CHAPTER 14

Destined to Win

You are Destined to Win

*Y*OU ARE DESTINED to win, God has a destiny for you and that is to be victorious in every area of your life, to overcome every obstacle, to be more than a conqueror. As Christians we should not have to live a defeated life, run over by the enemy, overcome with the struggles of life, conquered by the enemy.

> *I know the plans that I think toward you, thoughts of peace and not of evil, to give you a future and a hope. (Jeremiah 29:11 KJV)*

God has a plan for you to succeed in life and the enemy has a plan for you to fail. The devil is a sore loser. Jesus triumphed over him through his victory and what he accomplished through his death, burial, resurrection and ascension into heaven. In order to become more than a conqueror in life there must be an opponent to overcome.

We have an enemy whose only desire is to see God's people lose in life.

If you want to succeed in life there are three areas that you will have to develop in. First you must know the word of God, through it you come to know Jesus and through Jesus you come to know the Father. The word of God is what will teach you how to become an overcomer and help you to succeed in life.

What does it take to live a victorious life? And what does it take to become an overcomer and not be overcome? Maybe you are thinking, God cannot use me, I am not talented, I am not an anointed singer or teacher, I am just me. God is not looking for talent or ability, He is looking for availability. He is looking for available vessels he can use to confound the wise. You will be astonished at what God can do with you when you make yourself available to him.

We must see our self the way God sees us. One can never go forward while looking back. The Apostle Paul found that out, he said this one thing I do, forgetting what lies behind.

Three Things You Must Know so you can succeed in your walk with God

I am going to show you three important things we must know and understand if we want to win in life. The bible tells us that it is God working in you, but then it also tells us that we are workers together with God. *For it is God who*

*works in you both to will and to do for His good pleasure.
(Philippians 2:13 NKJV)*

> *For we are God's fellow workers; You are God's
> field, you are God's building.*
>
> *(1 Corinthians 3:9 NKJV)*

1. **You must know God and His word**
2. **You must know who you are in Christ and what he has done for you**
3. **Know your enemy**

It is very important that we develop a personal relationship with the Lord and the only way we can do that is through the knowledge of his word, because it's through the word of God that we come to know who Jesus is and what he accomplished in his life on the earth through his death, burial and resurrection, and also his ascension into heaven. It is only through the word of God and knowing Jesus that we become acquainted with our heavenly Father. God is our creator. *(Genesis 1:1 KJV) In the beginning God created the heaven and the earth.* The bible also informs us that God created man in his image, male and female he created them. He created them with authority to exercise it on the earth, to be fruitful and to multiply and to replenish the earth. *(Genesis 1:26 KJV)*

God placed us here on this earth with purpose. The enemy of our soul is the one who wants to destroy everything

God created. That is why we have the account in *(Genesis chapter 3)* of how subtle the enemy is, and how he deceived Eve in order to get her to eat of the fruit that God had commanded them not to eat of. The enemy has always wanted to be in charge, but God had a plan to redeem mankind even before the foundation of the world.

> *For God so loved the world, that he gave his only begotten Son, that whosoever believes in Him should not perish but have everlasting life. (John 3:16 KJV)*

God loved us in our sin because he understood that we in ourselves could never be righteous by works, in our fallen state.

Eve got in trouble in the Garden of Eden when the enemy came to her and suggested that it was ok to eat of the fruit of the tree of the knowledge of good and evil because it would make her wise like God. It was her imagination that got her off track because she began to look at the tree and see that it did not look evil, in fact it looked like it would be good enough to eat and it would also make her wise. If she had stopped there it would not have gotten her into trouble, but she let her imagination get the best of her and she reached out and took the fruit and ate and gave to her husband with her. They immediately began to have feelings they had not experienced before. The first thing they noticed was that they were naked and tried to sew fig leaves together to cover themselves. When God asked Adam where are you? Adam said I was afraid because I was naked, and I hid myself.

He not only realized that they were naked, he experienced shame for the first time. Shame separated them from the presence of God. The bible says before they disobeyed God, they were naked, and they were not ashamed. The devil always wants to cause one to fear and to be ashamed. Then we see where blame began. Adam blamed God for the woman God gave him and Eve blamed the devil. The devil did not have anything to say because he is a deceiver and a liar. You can read the account in *(Genesis chapter 3)*.

We must understand that there are consequences to every wrong we do and that we have an enemy who is set on destroying us any way he can, and because we don't know our enemy many times we blame God for things the enemy is doing.

It is not what you or I have done that determines whether we are accepted by God or not. It is what he has done, Knowing the word you will not have to live a life of trying to please God and feeling condemned because you failed. You will not find yourself falling into temptation, then feeling guilty. You will be able to recognize temptation when it comes. The bible says God will make a way of escape but most of us fail to recognize it, if we could just recognize it, we would not fall into it. It is not a sin to be tempted, it becomes sin when we enter it, and then we are overcome by it.

> *No temptation has overtaken you except such as*
> *is common to man; but God is faithful, who will*
> *not allow you to be tempted beyond what you are*

*able, but with the temptation will also make a way
of escape, that you may be able to bear it.*

(1 Corinthians 10:13 NKJV)

Know your enemy, know who he is, know how he operates

*The thief does not come except to steal, and to kill,
and to destroy. I have come that they may have
life, and that they may have it more abundantly.*
(John 10:10 NKJV)

Here we see the difference between the character of God and that of our enemy. The enemy has not changed, throughout the ages he is still stealing, killing and destroying. It has worked since the beginning of time. Human beings still fall for his lies and deceptions. That is another reason we must know what the bible says about him. Did you know that many churches do not teach that we have an enemy? Therefore, God gets blamed for many things he is not guilty of. The bible tells us we are not to be ignorant of Satan's devices.

*Lest Satan should get an advantage of us, we are
not ignorant of Satan's devices.*

(2 Corinthians 2:11 NKJV)

Know Who You Are in Christ

If you do not know who you are in Christ, the enemy will turn you every which way but loose. He has a difficult time trying to fool Christians who know the word, know the Lord and know who they are in Christ. I recommend reading the book of Ephesians. In it you will find that God loves you not only does he love you, but he has accepted you and adopted you, you are blessed. God approves of you, how much more approval do you need? If God approves of us and he loves us, why are we so concerned by what others think of us. The only approval we need is that of God. The only opinion that matters is God's opinion of us.

God created you in his image and made you just the way he wanted you. He made you unique, there is no one else like you. Each one of us is uniquely created. It is the enemy who mars our image so that we do not see our self the way God wants us to see our self.

In order to understand how the enemy operates, we must go back to the Garden of Eden and see how the enemy operates. God created Adam and Eve in his image, then the enemy came into the garden and convinced Eve that God had left something out, something he was not telling them. (*Genesis 3:4-5* KJV) That is how subtle the enemy works. First thing he did was ask the question, Has God said? always trying to undermine the word of God. After she tells him what God said, He twisted what God said and said, you will not die if you eat of the fruit (my paraphrase).

How many times do we fall for that same thing? How many times did he tell you, it is not going to hurt if you do it just this once? It will not hurt you to try drugs if you just do it one time. He never tells you the end-result, he never tells you it could ruin your life or worse, end it.

You have believed the lies that people have said and what the devil says so why not believe what God says and trust God instead. Trust his word because God will never fail you. God is always with you. He will never leave you nor forsake you. (Hebrews *13:5. NKJV)* God gives hope to the hopeless.

Let the word of God be the mirror that you look in to and see yourself the way he sees you. The Bible says we are being changed from glory to glory, changed into his image, the image he has of you and me. Before we can see ourselves, the way God sees us, we must remove the veil that has been over our face, that has kept us from seeing the person we really are, created in his image.

(2 Corinthians 3:18 NKJV)

But we all, with unveiled face, beholding as in a mirror the glory of the Lord, are being transformed into the same image from glory to glory, just as by the Spirit of the Lord.

Isn't that awesome? When we look in the mirror of God's word, we are being changed. God's word has the power to change us, to take the ashes of our past and make something beautiful out of what we thought was lost. Out of the ashes, beauty shall rise!!

Trust the word of God and stop believing the lies of the enemy. Believe that you are who God says you are, and you can do what God's word says you can do. Put off the lies that you believed and fill your mind with the word of God, in so doing you will begin to see yourself being transformed from glory to glory.

God created you special and unique, no matter what it may look like now, there is a hidden treasure waiting to be revealed and beauty can be found in the ashes of your life, that will transform the way you think and the way you have been seeing yourself.

God makes everything beautiful in its time.

Printed in the United States
By Bookmasters